An estimated two hundred photographers rushed to Johnstown to record what was clearly the greatest natural disaster of the nineteenth century. Carrying ponderous box cameras, tripods, black hoods, flash powder, and other paraphernalia, the photographers clambered over the debris to photograph the wreckage from all angles. Most of them were making collections of stereographs and lantern slides, the popular precursors of today's slide show. Though sometimes nuisances to the rescue and cleanup efforts, the photographers created a rich document of the aftermath of the Great Flood.

Facing page, top left
One of the most frequently photographed subjects was the Schultz house. The flood carried the house several blocks and speared it with a tree, roots dangling thirty feet above the ground, but all six occupants survived.

THE JOHNSTOWN FLOOD OF 1889

The Tragedy of the Conemaugh

by Paula and Carl Degen

Library of Congress card catalog number 84-10103.
ISBN 1-888213-56-6

Text and photo selection by Paula and Carl Degen, Harpers Ferry, West Virginia.
Photo reproduction by Ted Jones, Falls Church, Virginia.

Designed by Winston G. Potter.
Produced by Publishing Center for Cultural Resources, NYC.
Manufactured in the USA.

The authors and publisher thank the staffs of the Cambria County Library, the Johnstown Flood Museum, and the Library of Congress for providing access to the photographic collections in their care. Our special appreciation goes to Richard Burkert, executive director of the Johnstown Flood Museum, whose knowledge of the 1889 flood greatly assisted this project.

Credits
Johnstown Flood Museum: 5; 9; 10 top right and bottom; 11; 40 top left; 45 left; 48 bottom; 50 top and bottom left; 57 top left and bottom right; 58 top; 60 bottom left; 63 top; back inside cover.

Cambria County Library: cover; inside front cover, top and bottom left; 1 top and bottom right; 10 top left; 15 through 24; 27 top right and bottom left; 28 bottom; 29; 31; 34; 36 top; 37 top; 38 top; 39 top; 40 bottom left and right; 42; 43; 44 bottom; 45 right; 46; 47 top; 48 top; 49 top and bottom right; 51; 52; 56; 59; 60 top left; 63 bottom.

Library of Congress: inside front cover, right; 1 left; 25; 27 top left and bottom right; 28 top; 33; 36 bottom; 37 bottom; 38 bottom; 39 bottom; 41; 44 top; 47 bottom; 49 bottom left; 50 top and bottom right; 55; 57 top right and bottom left; 58 bottom; 60 right; 61; back cover.

For Further Reading

Many books about the Johnstown Flood were written by survivors of the tragedy and by journalists who rushed to the scene. Among the most reliable and readable of these contemporary accounts are:

Beale, The Reverend David J. *Through the Johnstown Flood: By A Survivor*. Philadelphia: Hubbard Brothers, 1890.

McLaurin, J. J. *The Story of Johnstown*. Harrisburg: James M. Place, 1890.

McLaurin, a newsman from Harrisburg, visited Johnstown immediately after the flood and recorded vivid descriptions of the devastation. Excerpts from his book, especially his street-by-street description of the center city, have been used frequently to caption contemporary photographs in this book.

Of the secondary sources describing the 1889 flood, the doctoral dissertation by the late Nathan D. Shappee is the only known scholarly study, but it is as yet unpublished.

Shappee, Nathan D. *A History of Johnstown and the Great Flood of 1889: A Study of Disaster and Rehabilitation*. 1940 Dissertation on file at the University of Pittsburgh.

A more accessible and popularized history of the flood, the following is particularly recommended for its portrayals of people. Well researched and written, this is the best overall source.

McCullough, David G. *The Johnstown Flood*. New York: Simon & Schuster, 1968.

Also recommended are:

O'Connor, Richard. *Johnstown: The Day the Dam Broke*. Philadelphia: J. B. Lippincott Co., 1957. A latter-day journalistic approach to the flood story.

Strayer, Harold H. and London, Irving. *A Photographic Story of the 1889 Johnstown Flood*. Johnstown, Pa.: The Camera Shop, 1964. Based on Mr. London's extensive private collection of Johnstown photographs.

Johnstown, Pennsylvania, was an internationally known manufacturing center in the spring of 1889. Thriving on its iron and steel industry, Johnstown seemed to epitomize the growth and prosperity of post-Civil War America. New buildings were going up everywhere; every day new people arrived—many with foreign-sounding names and dialects—to work in the factories; new inventions were introducing ways for cleaner, healthier, and more comfortable living. Johnstown already had paved streets, fire hydrants, indoor plumbing, electric lights, and—as of January—even telephone service in some homes. Its newest hotel, the Hulbert House on Clinton Street, boasted an elevator and steam heat.

Like the nation as a whole, Johnstown radiated optimism. That spring of 1889 marked the centennial of the U.S. Constitution. The young nation had survived the test of civil war, and in the twenty-four years since the war's end, America had been rebuilding and expanding Westward, primarily with Johnstown steel rails, barbed wire, plowshares, and machinery. As the citizens of Johnstown gathered on May 30 to honor the war dead with the annual Memorial Day parade and speeches, they must have thought the future looked particularly bright for their town. Not only was the hotel new, but there were two new blocks of business buildings on Main Street, a new railroad station, and a new hospital. Their town already had a handsome city park, a library, two opera houses, numerous churches, fashionable mansions, a roller skating rink, a street railway out to neighboring boroughs, a baseball team, and a population of over 10,000 for Johnstown proper. Adding the suburban boroughs, which were stacked along the narrow valley and hillsides around Johnstown, the population that May totaled nearly 30,000.

Some people in the Memorial Day gathering could remember when Johnstown was quite a different place. It had been a tiny rural village during the first three decades of the century. When the State of Pennsylvania made it an important town on the route of the new canal system between Philadelphia and Pittsburgh, Johnstown became the western point where canal boats were transferred to and from the Allegheny Portage Railroad as part of the state's impressive canal and rail system through the mountains. From the time the Portage Railroad opened in 1834, Johnstown bustled with the arrival and departure of boats and trains. The canal meant prosperity and expansion for Johnstown, attracting travelers, skilled craftsmen, professionals, merchants, and other tradesmen to the area.

The canal era ended abruptly in 1854 when the Pennsylvania Railroad completed its own trackage across the state. Johnstown fared better than some towns that had depended upon the canal trade, for it became a terminal for the new rail system. By the late 1850s more than 28,000 tons of freight and 34,000 passengers were reported to have traveled through Johnstown in a single year.

At the same time, production of iron and steel from native ore deposits began to transform Johnstown from a transportation point to a major industrial center. There had been fledgling attempts to develop the area's abundant coal, ore, and limestone deposits as early as 1809, but by the 1850s the new railroad system, together with the wealth of natural resources, promised an expansive industry. In 1855, Daniel J. Morrell arrived in Johnstown to take charge of the Cambria Iron Company. The company prospered under his leadership, and at the time of the Civil War was the largest iron-producing center in the country. The war meant flush times for the iron industry. Furthermore, Morrell was quick to recognize the importance of the new Bessemer technique for converting iron into steel, and after the war, the Cambria Company invested heavily in Bessemer equipment. In 1867, the Cambria mill rolled out the first Bessemer rails made in the United States, and within a few years the Cambria Company was the largest steel producer in the country, if not the world.

What was good for the Cambria Iron Company was good for Johnstown. Under the patronage of the company, Johnstown had grown from a single borough of 1,300 people in 1850 to the mercantile center for a cluster of boroughs that had a combined population of about 15,000 in 1880—and nearly double that only nine years later. The Cambria Company and its subsidiaries were by far the principal employers and the reason for the area's extraordinary growth. More than 7,000 men were on the Cambria payroll in 1889.

Smokestacks sixteen to nineteen feet in diameter rose seventy-five feet high above the brick buildings. The rolling mill was nearly 2,000 feet long. The main works sprawled over sixty acres of bottomland at Johnstown. The company also owned coal mines, coke ovens, and gas pipelines. It operated sixty-eight miles of railroad and mine tracks above its works. It was the largest landowner in Cambria County, having bought thousands of acres for coal holdings. Enormous farms occupied much of this land, growing hay to feed the animals used in the mills and mines. The Cambria Company also owned several subsidiary industries, chief among them being the Gautier Steel Company where Cambria Link Barbed Wire was made.

Johnstown depended on the Cambria Company, and so did the boroughs and villages around it. Conemaugh Borough, at the eastern end of Johnstown proper, the location of the Gautier Works, was thickly settled with a population of 4,000 some distance up Green Hill. Prospect, on the high hill north of Johnstown, had 800 residents, most of whom rented houses from the company. The main rolling mills, foundries, machine shops, blast furnaces, and other works of the Cambria Company were located in Millville, in which almost 2,700 people lived. Cambria City, just across the Conemaugh River from the mills, also depended on the payroll of the Cambria Company; its population was 2,900. Woodvale had a Cambria Company chemical works, woolen mill, tannery, flouring mill, brick works—and a population of 1,200. East Conemaugh, built around the railroad yards, had 1,700 residents, and Franklin, a residential community, had over 600. Other boroughs and villages—Kernville, Morrellville, Coopersdale, Moxham—were all more or less linked to the Cambria Company.

The company influenced most aspects of life for people in and around Johnstown. Nearly everyone traded at the huge Wood, Morrell and Company, which was the department store for the Cambria Company. The store employed more than 400 people in its grand three-story brick structure on Washington Street. It offered meat from livestock raised on the iron company's farms, flour and cereal products from the Woodvale flouring mill, cloth from the Woodvale woolen mills, and an amazing variety of other merchandise. The Cambria Company had built the new hospital and the new library for the town, and even ran a night school offering free classes for employees. Although work in the mills and factories was hot, hard, and dangerous, the company looked out for the well-being of its employees and property.

But there was a careless disregard for the welfare of the land—a characteristic of this period of America's development. Natural resources were abundant, and in the haste to expand and profit, industrialists gave little thought to the scars they left on the landscape. At a time when human ingenuity could conquer the highest mountains and the deepest seas, there was an arrogant lack of respect for the power and vagaries of nature.

Homes and businesses crowded every available part of the valley. A pre-flood panorama shows central Johnstown, the Stony Creek, and the gap through which the flood waters rushed.

Man and nature both were villains in the drama that occurred at Johnstown in 1889. When rain began to fall at the conclusion of Memorial Day ceremonies, no one in the crowd anticipated the event that propelled Johnstown to worldwide notoriety. But by the end of the next day, the complicity of man and nature raised havoc on Johnstown and the surrounding communities, and this place became the scene of the most devastating flood in America's history.

At the center of a great valley in the Alleghenies and bounded by steep hills rising 500 to 1,000 feet, Johnstown rests at the confluence of two mountain streams. The Little Conemaugh flows swiftly in from the east. From its head near the coal town of Lilly on Allegheny Mountain, the Little Conemaugh drops

---

Top, left to right
Central Park was the pride of the city—a handsome oasis in the center of the main business district. It had lush lawns, cinder paths, gaslights, and an ornate fountain. The flood left debris so high in the park that survivors could climb across it into second floor windows of remaining buildings.

More than twenty congregations had churches in Johnstown at the time of the flood. The First Methodist Episcopal Church at Franklin and Locust streets, fronting the park, was one of the largest, having $100,000 in property and a membership of 850 in 1889. This sturdy stone building withstood the flood, parting the waters to protect the parsonage and nearby buildings.

The Parke Opera House, on Main Street near Franklin, was one of two opera houses in Johnstown. Already too small for the entertainment needs of the growing city, it was used for stores at the time of the flood.

Bottom, left to right
Cambria Iron Works' main mills. The stone bridge was the scene of one of the flood's most tragic episodes.

The Stenger Dry Goods Store on Main Street, one of Johnstown's many businesses in the 1880s.

down a narrow, winding, high-walled gorge to Johnstown, descending from 2,300 feet to 1,200 feet in less than twenty miles. At Johnstown, Stony Creek flows in from the south. The two rivers join at "the Point" to form the Conemaugh, which in turn flows west and north toward Pittsburgh.

For years, the town and its industries encroached on the natural surroundings. Factories and dwellings occupied every available piece of flat land and climbed up the accessible parts of the hillsides. But the mountains impeded expansion, and when the industries and towns needed more land, they took it from the rivers—filling in, narrowing the banks, dumping mill refuse and other waste onto the hard rock riverbeds. The factories had voracious appetites for natural resources. The hills surrounding Johnstown already had been denuded of native timber—first in the 1840s and '50s for fueling the iron furnaces and the railroads, then in the 1870s for the manufacture of barrel shooks and staves. By the 1880s, the original forests had disappeared, causing serious runoffs from spring thaws and heavy rains.

The mills and factories had a large appetite for clean water, so as the industrial area expanded, they took advantage of the mountain streams that fed the Conemaugh. By 1889, there were already six dams of varying sizes to supply the estimated 71 million gallons of water Johnstown's mills and homes used every day. The dams hindered the natural courses of the rivers. Any one of them could have endangered the towns below; but the dam that posed the greatest threat was one at South Fork that had been built many years earlier for the state's canal system.

When Pennsylvania's "Main Line" system of canals and railroads began operation in the 1830s, it became clear that its Western Division did not have enough water to maintain the level of the canal from Johnstown to Blairsville in the dry summer sea-

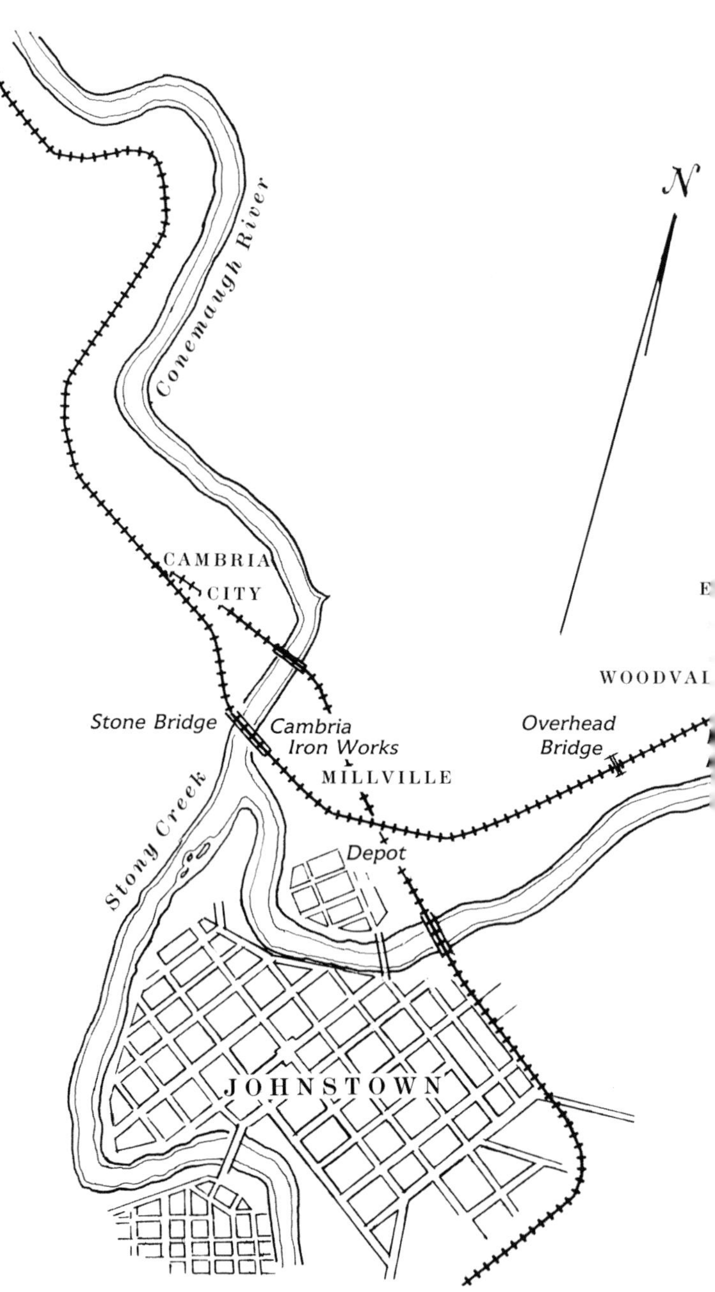

The fourteen miles from Lake Conemaugh to Johnstown were devastated by the flood. Map redrawn from an 1889 original by Alex. Y. Lee.

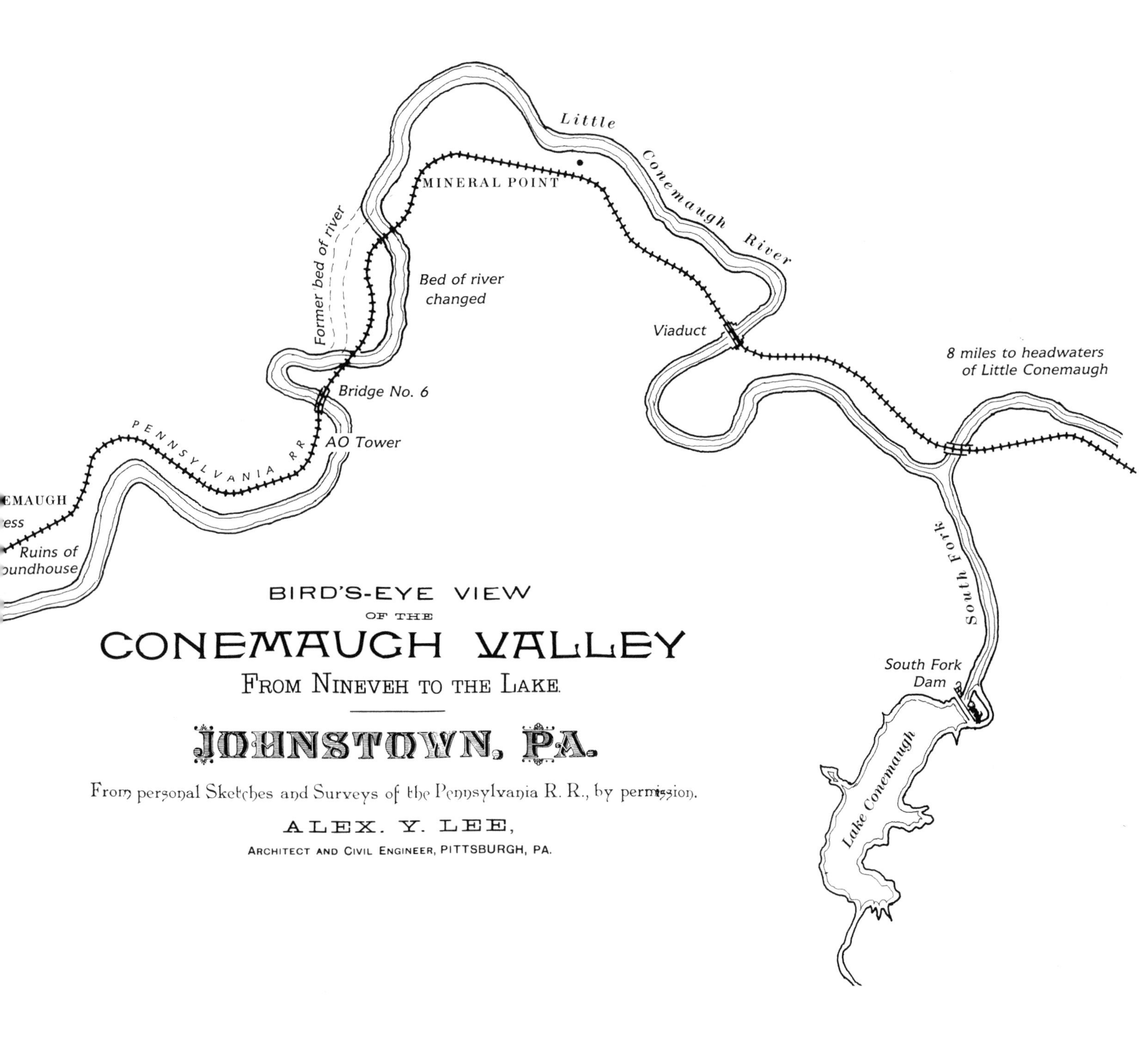
Little Conemaugh River
MINERAL POINT
Former bed of river
Bed of river changed
Viaduct
8 miles to headwaters of Little Conemaugh
Bridge No. 6
AO Tower
PENNSYLVANIA R.R.
EMAUGH
ess
Ruins of
oundhouse
South Fork
South Fork Dam
Lake Conemaugh
BIRD'S-EYE VIEW
OF THE
CONEMAUGH VALLEY
FROM NINEVEH TO THE LAKE
JOHNSTOWN, PA.
From personal Sketches and Surveys of the Pennsylvania R. R., by permission.
ALEX. Y. LEE,
ARCHITECT AND CIVIL ENGINEER, PITTSBURGH, PA.

son. In 1839 work began on a storage reservoir on the western slope of Allegheny Mountain, at the south fork of the Little Conemaugh. Lack of funds suspended construction for a ten-year period, but in 1853 the South Fork Dam and Western Reservoir were completed.

The project had cost the state more than $166,000 and the results were impressive. Some sources say the earthen dam was the largest work of its kind in the world, and that the reservoir was the largest manmade lake in the United States. By all accounts, it was an engineering masterpiece.

A mound of earth 931 feet long, the South Fork Dam towered 72 feet high, was 272 feet thick at the base, and had a wagon road across the top. Engineers constructed the dam carefully of successive layers of clay earth, each layer packed and "puddled" under a skim of water to make it watertight. The puddled-clay core was supported on both sides by stone riprap. Some of the rocks lining the outer face were so large they required three teams of horses to move them into place.

Five cast iron pipes, each two feet in diameter and set in a stone arch culvert, pierced the base of the dam. These pipes discharged water from the reservoir into the South Fork to flow down the Little Conemaugh and feed the canal at Johnstown, some fourteen miles away. The flow through these pipes was regulated from a wooden tower nearby.

The southwestern end of the dam was anchored to the hillside by a twenty-foot-high stone wall. To prevent the water behind the dam from rising to the top and flowing over the crest, a spillway was cut through the solid rock that anchored the northeastern end to the hillside. The spillway was seventy-two feet wide and its bottom was nine feet below the crest of the dam.

The water impounded by this massive structure in 1853 covered nearly 425 acres and was fifty feet deep at the dam. But even as the first waters filled in behind the South Fork Dam, events elsewhere in the state sealed the fate of the canal system, and by February 1854, when the Pennsylvania Railroad sent the first train over the Alleghenies without using inclined planes, the Portage road was obsolete. Three years later the Pennsylvania Railroad purchased the state's "Main Line" at auction and became the new owner of the entire system, including the Portage Railroad, South Fork Dam, and the Western Reservoir.

Having no use for the dam, the railroad did nothing to maintain it. Except for some commotion in 1862, the dam and reservoir were largely ignored for the eighteen years that the railroad owned them. Now and then people in the valley of the Conemaugh voiced concern about the huge dam 404 feet over their heads on the high mountain slope. On July 18, 1862, the *Cambria Tribune* reported that the canal reservoir was in ". . . dangerous condition. A portion of the arch in the breast wall has fallen, leaving but a feeble support at that point for the immense body of water behind it. Should the dam give way suddenly, as it is likely to do in the case of a heavy rain . . . the consequences would be serious."

A little over a week later, the first major break in the dam did occur. On July 26, after a heavy rain, the stone culvert collapsed and 200 feet of the dam washed out. Fortunately it was the dry season, and water levels were low in the reservoir and the stream beds below. Furthermore, a watchman at the dam opened the valves just before the break to relieve pressure, and the reservoir drained slowly over an eleven-hour period. Although news of the break caused considerable alarm among people living in the valley, they suffered little damage.

The railroad did not repair the break and soon abandoned the upper Western Division of the canal entirely. No one paid attention to the dry lakebed except a few farmers who grazed their cattle and sheep where grass grew along the slopes. In 1875 the railroad sold its "white elephant" to Congressman John Reilly of Altoona for $2,500. Reilly did nothing with the South Fork Reservoir for the four years he held it, and in 1879 he sold the property for only $2,000 to his friend Benjamin F. Ruff. By then the wooden tower that was used to control the pipes had burned to the ground, and the iron pipes themselves had been removed from the base of the dam and sold for scrap.

Ruff had plans for the former reservoir. The location was ideal for an exclusive mountain resort where club members could escape from the grimy heat of Pittsburgh in the summer. The South Fork Fishing and Hunting Club of Pittsburgh was chartered in November 1879, with Ruff as a principal stockholder and its first president. The following spring, reconstruction began on the South Fork Dam and Western Reservoir, which the club renamed "Lake Conemaugh."

Ruff, who had no experience in waterworks or dam construction, employed Edward Pearson of Pittsburgh as foreman and superintendent of the reconstruction. Pearson, an employee of a freight-hauling company, had neither engineering credentials nor experience in waterworks. The South Fork Fishing and Hunting Club would be forever censured for the fact that "at no time during the process of rebuilding the dam was any engineer whatever, young or old, good or bad, known or unknown, engaged on or consulted as to the work . . ." (*Engineering News and American Railway Journal*, June 15, 1889). Without a doubt, the club's changes in the dam's original structure contributed to the dam's failure in 1889.

The club set about repairing the old 1862 break and making the lake into a fish preserve. Leaks at the base of the dam were patched with hay, leaves, manure—whatever was at hand. The five holes where the sluice pipes had been were closed with hemlock piling, and the culvert gap was covered with rock. Earth was dumped into the breach without any attempt to water and ram it, and the mound was faced with loose stone instead of heavy boulders. The new work settled until the center of the dam

The South Fork Fishing and Hunting Club filled the culvert (near center of this 1887 photo) and lowered the crest of the dam for a carriage road.

The club installed wire screens and nail-studded logs to keep fish from escaping Lake Conemaugh— here, two years before the flood.

was only a few feet higher than the bottom of the spillway. According to reports of residents who observed the repairs, the height of the dam was lowered by two feet to make the crest wide enough for a two-lane carriage road, and there appeared to be a sag in the center. This meant that if the lake started running over the top of the dam, the center would be the point of greatest pressure.

In addition to removing the sluice pipes and filling in the holes, the club made other changes to keep fish from escaping. Disregarding the purpose of the spillway, which was to prevent water from rising higher than the crest of the dam, the club built two trestle bridges across it, thereby obstructing the free spillage of water. Fishguards of heavy wire screen were fastened between the supports of one of the bridges, which promised to be another obstruction, especially if the screens became clogged with debris. Above these fishguards an elevated screen kept fish from leaping onto the bridge or the wall—and, in case these were not enough, nail-studded logs were attached to the bridge and floated on the water in zig-zag fashion to keep fish away from the spillway. Thus, the obstacles that impounded the sportsmen's fish also hampered the flow of water; without the discharge pipes to lower the water level at will, the club had no control mechanism in the event of an emergency.

The slipshod manner of this repair work did not go unnoticed by residents of the valley below. While construction was in progress, Daniel Morrell, general manager of the Cambria Iron Company, sent John Fulton, a trained geologist and engineer, to the site to report on the quality of the repairs. Morrell, who had supervised the construction of several small dams put in near Johnstown by the water company, had reason for concern. After all, his company had more than $50 million in property along the Valley of the Conemaugh.

Fulton reported to Morrell in a letter dated November 26, 1880, that he did not believe the work "was being done in a careful and substantial manner, or with the care demanded in a large structure of this kind. . . ." Fulton's report continued:

> There appear to me two serious elements of danger in the dam:
>
> 1st. The want of a discharge pipe to reduce or take the water out of the dam for needed repairs.
>
> 2nd. The unsubstantial method of repair, leaving a large leak, which appears to be cutting the new embankment. As the water cannot be lowered, the difficulty arises of reaching the source of the present destructive leaks. At present there is 40 feet of water in the dam, when the full head of 60 feet is reached, it appears to me to be only a question of time until the former cutting is repeated. Should this break be made during a season of flood, it is evident that considerable damage would ensue along the line of the Conemaugh.

Benjamin Ruff disputed Fulton's findings and wrote to Morrell on December 2: ". . . you and your people are in no danger from our enterprise." But Morrell was still concerned, and on the 22nd offered to help bear the cost of a major overhaul of the dam:

> We do not wish to put any obstruction in the way of your accomplishing your object in the reconstruction of the dam, but we much protest against the erection of a dam at that place, that will be a perpetual menace to the lives and property of those residing in the upper valley of the Conemaugh from its insecure construction. In my judgement there should have been provided some means by which the water could be let out of the dam in case of trouble, and I think that you will find it necessary to provide an outlet pipe or gate before any engineer could pronounce the job a safe one. If this dam could be securely reconstructed with a safe means of driving off the water in case any weakness manifests itself . . . this company would be willing to cooperate with you in the work, and contribute liberally toward making the dam absolutely safe.

Ruff refused Morrell's offer and the reconstruction proceeded. Both Ruff and Morrell died before subsequent events proved the significance of their exchange of letters.

In 1881 the club completed repair work on the dam and shipped 1,000 black bass from Lake Erie to stock the new Lake Conemaugh. The lake now covered 500 acres and was between sixty and sixty-five feet deep at the dam. It was nearly three miles long and as much as a mile wide at spots.

A large three-story wooden clubhouse and several spacious cottages in the popular "Queen Anne" style of the day welcomed members to their new summer retreat. Sixty members were on the roster in the first season, each paying an initiation fee of $800. They were among the wealthiest and most prominent financiers of the time: Andrew Carnegie, John W. Chalfant, J. K. Ewing, Henry C. Frick, Philander Knox, Andrew Mellon, Henry Phipps, Jr., to name a few. Each member was permitted two weeks' accommodation for his family at the clubhouse, which had forty-seven bedrooms and a dining hall with seating for 150. The cottages nearby, some with as many as seventeen rooms, were owned by members who preferred more privacy.

For the next nine summers, the club's seventy acres of land and 500-acre lake posed quite a contrast to the steamy industrial center in the valley below. The setting was spectacular. As guests rode from the South Fork depot in their carriages along the crest of the dam they saw the face of the massive dam drop down to the valley on their right, and they looked across a grand expanse of clear mountain lake bordered by woods and meadows on their left. All summer long, parasols and fancy frocks graced the boardwalks and verandas along the lakeshore. Sailboats, canoes and rowboats, even two steam yachts, dotted the lake. Fish and game were abundant. Although not so ostentatious as Newport or Saratoga or other summering spots for the elite, South Fork was a favorite retreat for those who could afford its pleasures. In 1889 the membership numbered sixty-eight; there were twenty private cottages along the shores, and the staff at the clubhouse expected two hundred guests that summer.

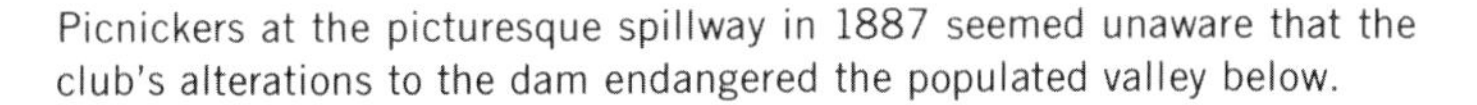

Picnickers at the picturesque spillway in 1887 seemed unaware that the club's alterations to the dam endangered the populated valley below.

The spillway emptied with the rest of Lake Conemaugh, leaving little of the setting that once attracted club members.

Despite frequent talk that the dam was unsafe, it withstood rains that flooded the Conemaugh Valley nearly every spring. The floods in 1885, 1887, and 1888 had been particularly bad—they seemed to get worse each year. And each year rumors circulated about the dam breaking. But people grew tired of hearing about a disaster that never happened, and some people—influential people—did not believe that the town would suffer much damage even if the dam did break. After all, it was a long way away. Besides, some of the most awesome and powerful men in the country owned the dam. They would not let it break.

Speculating on what might happen if indeed the great dam did go, George Swank, the editor of the *Johnstown Tribune*, implied there was no cause for alarm because the dam would go to pieces gradually. On June 30, 1887, he maintained that the breaking of the embankment would not affect Johnstown to any considerable degree unless it "occurred in conjunction with a great flood in the Conemaugh Valley, which is one of the possibilities not worth worrying about." Two years later, Swank was marooned in his office at the *Tribune* by the heaviest rainstorm in anyone's memory, writing an editorial intended for May 31: "It is idle to speculate what would be the result if this tremendous body of water—three miles long—a mile wide in places, and sixty feet deep at the breast at normal stage—should be thrown into the already submerged Valley of the Conemaugh." That piece was not published until June 14, for even as he wrote, the desperate efforts of workmen at the site could not keep the waters of Lake Conemaugh from flowing over the crest of the dam.

"Perhaps it would interest you to know what we had in the way of a summer resort. In the first place there is a very fine clubhouse or hotel with forty-seven bed-rooms, well furnished; a nicely furnished office, a pool room, a parlor forty feet square, a dining room 40 × 60 feet, a well-furnished kitchen, bakery, cooling rooms, milk room, vegetable room, and everything to be found in a well-furnished hotel. We also have sixteen cottages . . . two fine steam yachts, four sailing boats, and about fifty sailing canoes and row boats. Of course, none of them are of any use up here now." [W. Y. Boyer, South Fork Club Superintendent, June 10, 1889] Photo taken in 1887.

The rain began to fall on Johnstown at about 4:00 P.M. Thursday as Memorial Day activities were concluding. The rain clouds, part of a massive system that caused violent storms and floods across the country, stalled over the mountains of Pennsylvania from late afternoon on May 30 until June 1 and pelted the area of the South Fork watershed with an unprecedented rainfall. An empty pail left out near the South Fork Dam during the night of May 30 contained eight inches of water the next morning. The ground was already saturated from spring thaws and unusually heavy rains. May had been the wettest month on record: nine and a half to twelve and a half inches of rain had fallen on the area between Harrisburg and McConnellsburg even before the deluge began on May 30. Because three inches of rain in this area ordinarily produced floods, people in towns along the swollen mountain streams were already moving carpets and furniture upstairs, preparing for high water.

At the South Fork Fishing and Hunting Club, a crew of workmen had just concluded a day of digging sewer trenches when the rain started. Col. E. J. Unger, president of the club; W. Y. Boyer, superintendent of the grounds; and John G. Parke, the new resident engineer; were there to observe and supervise the work. The rain turned into a heavy downpour during the night, and by early morning the men saw that the lake had risen two feet. By 7:00 A.M. the water, rising at a rate of ten to twelve inches an hour, stood only six feet from the top of the embankment. To survey the danger, Parke made his way to South Fork Creek where he saw that the stream, normally two feet deep, was a raging torrent, stripping branches from trees as high as six feet above the bank. By now Parke and the others had no doubt about the severity of the situation at the dam.

For the next few hours they worked feverishly to keep the lake from going over the crest, knowing that the earthen dam could not

Looking east toward the lake from the path of destruction. The photographer marked this photograph to show the height of the dam before the center section broke away.

withstand pressure on the top and outer face. In an effort to relieve the burden of water flowing through the spillway at the northeastern end of the dam, the work crew and some local farmers tried to create a second spillway at the southwestern end. The hard shale resisted their picks and they succeeded in digging a ditch only two feet wide and fourteen inches deep. Water immediately rushed into the new channel and scooped out a trench twenty-five feet wide and twenty inches deep. When Unger saw the futility of digging a new spillway, he directed the men to plow a line along the length of the embankment to try to make the wall higher, but this too proved futile.

Meanwhile, John Parke rode down to the village of South Fork about two miles away to warn people of the danger and to have a message sent to Johnstown. This was the first of three warnings telegraphed from village to village that afternoon, but it is not known whether the residents of the towns received the messages from the telegraph stations. Some people later stated that they had heard the warnings, but, like the story of the boy who cried "wolf" too many times, they thought this was just another false alarm.

The final warning from South Fork arrived in Johnstown at 2:45 P.M.: "THE DAM IS BECOMING DANGEROUS AND MAY POSSIBLY GO." The railroad agent in Johnstown telephoned the message to Hettie Ogle who operated the central telephone switchboard at the corner of Washington and Walnut. Most of the dozen or so subscribers to the new telephone system were already marooned by high water, which was four to ten feet in the streets of Johnstown by then. Hettie telephoned editor Swank at the *Tribune* to pass on the warning from South Fork.

"It was my fortune, after witnessing the unspeakable horrors at Johnstown, to be the first to traverse the whole length and breadth of the devastated region. . . . The visit to the dam disclosed how the water had carved a highway for itself in its exhaustless rage. Both wings of the dam were standing intact, mute, hoary, moss-grown testimonies to the superior work done by the first contractors. The newer portions had gone, leaving not a particle of refuse, so thorough was the destruction. . . . The proud lake had dwindled to a thread winding amid the loose stones and muddy deposits of a pretty brook. The cottages looked upon a slimy, oozing gully, no longer the silver expanse that had pleased the eye two days before. Off on the hillside . . . the clubhouse and residences . . . seemed to invite the guests who did not come. . . ." [J. J. McLaurin]

Swank, who was keeping a running account of the events of the day, noted:

At 3:00 o'clock, the town sat down with its hands in its pockets to make the best of a very dreary situation. All had got out of the reach of the flood that could and there was nothing to do but wait; and what impatient waiting it was anyone who has ever been penned in by a flood and has watched the river rising, and the night coming on, can imagine. . . .

At 3:15 the Central Telephone office called the *Tribune* up to say it had been informed . . . that the South Fork Reservoir was getting worse all the time and that the danger of its breaking was increasing momentarily. . . . (*Johnstown Tribune*, June 14, 1889)

It was the last message sent by Hettie Ogle. At 3:15 P.M.—that very moment—the South Fork Dam gave way.

The workers at Lake Conemaugh looked on in horror. Their last attempt to save the dam had failed. They had tried to remove the fishguards attached to the bridge over the spillway, but the heavy iron grids, clogged with debris, did not budge.

The water in the lake, nearly seven and a half feet above normal, began spilling over the dam's crest about 11:30 A.M. From then until 3:00 P.M. the water washed away at the outer

face of the embankment until the dam was so thin at one point that it could no longer withstand the pressure from the lake behind it. John Parke, one of the eyewitnesses, later said: "The dam did not break. It simply moved away." Another observer said: "The whole dam seemed to push out all at once. No, not a break, just one big push."

The impounded water of the lake rushed through the breach in the dam with such force that it pushed a 420-foot section of wall into the valley below. In less than forty-five minutes, the lake emptied itself, sending twenty million tons of water pounding down the sluice-like valley toward unsuspecting Johnstown, fourteen miles away, 404 feet below. J. P. Wilson of South Fork, aware of the deepening notch in the embankment, heard the rush of water escaping and ran to the railroad telegraph tower. The operator laughed at Wilson's message, "The dam is breaking. Look out!" but she agreed to send it to the next station at Mineral Point. Mineral Point never received Wilson's message. From then on, the deafening roar of raging water sounded the warning.

The people at the dam site watched, numbed, until the rush passed. Club superintendent Boyer later recalled: "Trees four feet in diameter, roots, branches, everything went before it like toys, and before it reached South Fork it was a dam of trees, and not of clay and stones as before. . . ." But from South Fork on down the narrow mountain valley, the thirty-to-forty-foot wave picked up heavier and ever more grisly cargo. Moving an aver-

The village of South Fork, the first stop on the flood's path of destruction. "When the fatal break in the dam occurred the skies wore a leaden hue, as if in mourning for the region about to experience a direful visitation. . . . Raindrops glistened on every leaf and blade of grass, nature's subsidy of tears over the approaching horror." [J. J. McLaurin]

The depot at South Fork was once the point where trains from Pittsburgh brought members of the South Fork Fishing and Hunting Club to begin their summer holiday in the mountains.

age forty miles per hour, it had the momentum to roll locomotives for almost a mile, to sweep buildings and bridges from their foundations, to crush anything in its path.

Engineers later calculated that the flood wave had a force equal to that of Niagara Falls. Had it descended without interruption, the flood would have moved with a velocity of 60 to 100 miles per hour and reached Johnstown in twenty-five minutes. But the flood took twice that long for the descent, because it was slowed, sometimes almost stopped, by friction in the narrow, curving channel of the Conemaugh.

The friction created by the debris and the rugged terrain caused the lowest part of the wave to move more slowly than the top, creating a violent downward smash, an enormous surf. Layers of water threw debris over the top of the main wave and pushed it downward; successive layers threw more water and more debris over the top. Witnesses described the flood wave as a "rolling ball," and houses, rocks, trees, rails, locomotives, telegraph poles, animals, and human bodies were caught up in its sphere. The ball of water moved fast enough to create a wind before it. The wind, the dark mist of spray and dust, and the thunderous sound of the grinding, crashing mass are what survivors remembered about the approach of the flood wave.

The wave claimed its first victims in the tiny village of South Fork. Located on a hillside where the South Fork branch meets the Little Conemaugh, the village was not in the direct path of the great wave, and suffered relatively little damage. When the rushing wave of lake water reached the mouth of the South Fork branch, it crashed full force against the mountain that forms the north bank of the Little Conemaugh River. The impact divided the wave, sending one part up the Little Conemaugh to the village, but the greater part started downriver. The backwash that swept over South Fork village carried the remains of an iron railroad bridge, swept from its pilings and twisted almost in half. Besides the bridge, the wave destroyed a planing mill, some twenty other buildings and houses, a coal tipple and the telegraph tower, but only four people were killed. Almost everyone in South Fork had heeded the warnings and sought safety.

Most of the water went down the Little Conemaugh, picking up freight cars, rails, ties, and railroad equipment along the way. The flood wave met its first major obstacle about a mile west of the South Fork. There the river entered a deep ravine where the narrowing valley walls forced the flood wave to a height of almost seventy-five feet.

The river's course turns sharply south, scribes a horseshoe turn, and flows north before heading westward again. The distance around the curve is more than a mile, but the distance across the neck is only 150 feet. The Pennsylvania Railroad followed the north bank of the river and crossed the neck in a deep cut. It went over the Little Conemaugh by the old Portage Railroad viaduct, a seventy-five-foot sandstone landmark that bridged the river gap with a single eighty-foot arch. The viaduct had withstood every flood in the valley for over fifty years.

The flood wave separated again when it reached the cut east of the viaduct. Part of the wave carried houses, railroad equipment, and logs through the cut and over the top of the viaduct. Another part took the longer path around the bend of the river, gathering its own cargo of debris, which then jammed in the huge arch. Meanwhile the wave that had earlier swept over the village of South Fork rejoined the main thrust. Flood lines indicated that the gathered waters were eighty-nine feet above the river bed and flowed nearly twenty feet deep over the top of the old viaduct. For a brief moment the wreckage created a second dam for Lake Conemaugh, but unable to endure the tremendous pressure, the bridge collapsed. Freed, the water exploded into the valley with renewed energy, leaving almost no trace of the viaduct.

Just below the viaduct, the river turns sharply and runs westward through the valley past Mineral Point. A village of fewer than two hundred people, its neat white frame houses sat in a row along a single street parallel to the river. Nearly everyone in the village worked either in the planing mill or the furniture factory owned by the Cambria Iron Company.

The telegraph operator at Mineral Point said he did not receive the message from South Fork about the dam breaking; his first warning was from people floating by in their houses. The flood wave would have claimed more than the sixteen lives it took at Mineral Point had not high water already forced most people to leave their homes. After the great wave, the survivors had little to return to. Twenty-six of the thirty-two houses in the village were completely destroyed, together with the factory, the mill, and other buildings. Where once each home had a little garden, the wave scraped the valley floor down to bare rock. The clock in the railroad tower stopped at 3:41 P.M., marking the exact time of the destruction of Mineral Point.

A mile and a half below Mineral Point, the force of the flood cut a new channel for the Little Conemaugh. Before the flood the river flowed close to the western bank of a narrow basin; but the great wave rounded the bend from Mineral Point and struck the side of a mountain with such force that the river was deflected to the eastern bank where it now flows.

The course of the river next forms an "S" curve flowing west, then east, then south, then west again. Swinging around the lower curve, the flood wave was thrown against the eastern bank, thus sparing a locomotive and work crew which were on the track on the west side. For more than twenty minutes, the

---

The remains of Mineral Point. "But what of the pretty hamlet nestling at the foot of the hills? . . . Thirty-two cosy abodes had ranged along a tongue of flat land, facing the creek and a street. . . . On came the turbid waters emitting a cloud of mist suggestive of the smoke of a burning forest or the dust of a whirlwind in the Sahara. . . . One minute cleared away twenty-six dwellings and the gardens surrounding them. . . . A barren waste, destitute of soil as a block of granite, marked the site of what had been an inviting spot. Dismal was the spectacle to those who knew Mineral Point in its tranquil repose." [J. J. McLaurin]

The massive Conemaugh Viaduct, a popular attraction in the Portage Railroad days, was only briefly an obstacle to the flood.

assistant-superintendent of the railroad and his men watched as the water bore through the river channel below what was known as the "AO" tower. The wave took with it every vestige of the old Portage Railroad for more than a mile. At the next bend it tore out the four-track embankment of the Pennsylvania Railroad, adding 2,000 feet of rails, ties, and ballast to the load of debris, and leaving behind only a sheer rock cliff.

Once past the curves below the AO tower, the flood gained the power and speed that characterized its thrust into the densely populated valley below. Until then, the progress of the wave had been intermittent. Jammed timber, earth, rock, and other debris would briefly check the forward movement, but then, with a seething, violent rush that threw trees into the air, the mass would move forward again with even greater speed. Except for the momentary impediment of the narrow valley above the borough of East Conemaugh, the wave now had a clear shot down to Johnstown.

East Conemaugh was the place where trains were made up for the arduous haul over the Allegheny Mountains. Most of its inhabitants worked for the railroad. In the yards that day there

The wreckage of the *Day Express* where twenty-two passengers lost their lives. The train was in the East Conemaugh yards when a locomotive whistle sounded the alarm. "There was no time for explanation and none was needed. . . . Already the roar of advancing waters filled the air. Those who first reached the platform saw wrecked houses, broken bridges, trees and rocks borne on a tidal wave just turning the bend three hundred yards away. Frantic exertions were made to escape to the protecting hills back of the station. . . . Some of the terrified passengers jumped or fell into the waters and drowned, the deluge from the reservoir overtaking them as they floundered in the ditch. A few of those who could not leave the train survived with painful bruises, a drenching and paralyzing fright, the waters rising half-way to the car-roofs. Several were caught in the deadly swirl as they tried to crawl under the vestibuled coaches of the second section, which lay on the inside track. It was the work of a moment to envelop the trains." [J. J. McLaurin]

were thirty-three locomotives, several freight cars, and three passenger trains, including two sections of the Day Express from Pittsburgh which had been detained because of washouts on the tracks ahead. In addition, there were machine shops, a sixteen-stall roundhouse, and other buildings and equipment.

At the eastern end of the yards, the work train of John Hess sat facing downstream waiting for orders. When Engineer Hess heard the roar of the approaching flood, he knew instinctively what was happening. He tied down the whistle and heroically sped his train into East Conemaugh. Had the track been clear, he probably would have continued his drive into Johnstown. As it was, he abandoned his engine in East Conemaugh only moments before the flood hit. The whistle continued its steady scream for several minutes more before being silenced by the flood. It was the only warning for people in East Conemaugh and neighboring boroughs, and those who were able fled to the hills.

The railroad yards of East Conemaugh on the north bank of the river and the lower rows of tenements of Franklin across the river on the south took the brunt of the wave's blow. Twenty-eight residents from the two boroughs and twenty-two passengers on the Day Express were killed. The roundhouse, turntable, machine shops, coal tipple, station house, rails, boxcars, engines and tenders (weighing as much as eighty tons), and an estimated 150 houses were now rolled into the wave. Some of the cars caught fire. Twenty-three locomotives were scattered about; one was carried 4,800 feet by the wave. One tender, ripped from its locomotive, was thrust against a tree with such force that the tender, not the tree, broke in half. With the addition of this weighty cargo, the wave bore down on the suburbs adjoining Johnstown.

Woodvale, a borough of just over one thousand people, gave little resistance to the crushing wave. Woodvale was the pride of the Cambria Iron Company, its model town, with charming white frame houses, tree-lined Maple Avenue—the most handsome street in the valley—and a streetcar line into Johnstown. When the flood finished with Woodvale, nothing remained save part of the walls of the woolen and flouring mills, and a span of a footbridge over the railway. In five minutes of terror, the flood wiped out every one of the 255 houses in the town proper, as well as a tannery, the streetcar shed with eighty-nine horses and thirty tons of hay, every tree and telegraph pole, every vestige of the railroad, and 314 people—about one out of every four who lived in the town.

At the western end of Woodvale stood the Gautier Steel Company, partly in Woodvale and partly in Conemaugh borough. A terrific geyser of steam went up when the wave hit the boilers of the Gautier works, and then the whole wireworks, with its massive furnaces and machinery, seemed to lift up and slide away with the water. The destruction of the Gautier works added to the mountain of debris miles of wire—some 200 rolls of steel cable and barbed wire weighing more than 200,000 pounds. The wave cut a broad swath of destruction through the borough of Conemaugh into Johnstown. The time was 4:10 P.M., not quite an hour since the dam had given way at South Fork.

The wave had built up such momentum that it pounded Johnstown with greater force than anywhere else. It took only about

---

"An ominous crash, and the round-house and nine heavy engines disappeared. Everything in the line of the flood was displaced or swallowed up. Locomotives were tossed aside and their tenders spirited off. . . . A Pullman coach rolled off and was crushed, a resident picking up one of its gas fixtures next day at the lower end of Woodvale. Mere playthings for the whirlpool, engines and cars were hidden beneath the timbers, brush, and dirt. Slaked by the water, a cargo of lime on the train between the sections of the express set two Pullman coaches blazing. Thus fire and flood combined to lend fresh horrors to the onslaught." [J. J. McLaurin]

Far right, top
"Locomotive 1309, a fifty-ton eight-wheeler, stood in its place, smoke curling from its stack, steam issuing from the safety-valve, and driftwood heaped up to the top of the headlight, the glass in which, by a curious fantasy of the flood, was not cracked." [J. J. McLaurin]

P. R. R.

Facing page
"In front of the woolen mill an iron bridge spanned the railroad tracks, the ends resting on stone piers of medium size. Wooden approaches on stout trestles connected it with either side, affording a convenient foot-way for persons desiring to cross the valley. Dreaming not of danger, forty or fifty people leaned on the railings to observe the rising waters. . . . The clouds of smoke-like mist and the noise of crunching houses admonished them to seek the hills with utmost dispatch. . . . By an extraordinary freak the iron span was spared, a skeleton network of rods and braces fluttering in mid-air. Bridges many times heavier had nourished the demolisher, yet this frail structure, built with no thought that a flood would ever try to lay it low, emerged unharmed." [J. J. McLaurin]

The remains at Woodvale with mud flats, once Franklin and Conemaugh, in the background. The iron bridge is seen here from afar. "From East Conemaugh and Franklin, renewing its energy at every step, the flood swooped upon Woodvale. The valley narrowed and the water reared its frowning crest higher as it advanced, stripping the earth bare in its vindictive passion. . . . Nothing was too small to escape its notice or too large for it to attack. Locomotives turned somersaults, and houses played leapfrog in the bosom of the merciless current, which churned them into battered iron and splintered wood to strew its trail with wreckage. Havoc ruled the hour and chaos was monarch of the day." [J. J. McLaurin]

Right
Two views of the remains of the Gautier Mills. "The Gautier Wire Mills and Steel Works . . . were soon licked up, the six or eight immense departments furnishing a morsel of which the flood made speedy work. Their demolition was complete, not one brick tarrying above the stone foundations. Heaps of sand entombed what machinery the ruthless water did not thrust from its moorings and grind to powder. Large rolls of barbed wire entangled with the rubbish and wound tightly about scores of the four hundred men, women and children who by this time were fighting for life in the turgid current. Held in the inflexible grip of the wire, fastened by timbers, or sinking from exhaustion, young and old met death in forms unutterably horrible." [J. J. McLaurin]

ten minutes to lay waste to the city. Washington Street took the initial impact—its buildings and shops were gone in an instant. From there the wave seemed to branch into several paths of destruction. One branch followed Jackson Street; one went down Clinton; and one swept down Franklin straight to Stony Creek. These thrusts first followed the north-south streets but then spread out to destroy other parts of the city. The water that rushed down Clinton tore through to Franklin Street, where, deflected by the Franklin Street Methodist Church, it went down Locust Street in one direction and across the city park in the other. Another wave tore a path from Franklin to Market. All around, brick buildings crumbled, while frame buildings were picked up by the swirling waters to be smashed to bits or simply carried away. Within a few moments nearly all the streets of Johnstown were rivers of debris rushing headlong for Stony Creek.

The main body of the wave, carrying the most wreckage, sped due west, razing everything in its path, until it slammed into the side of Westmont Hill, an impenetrable barrier rising nearly 550 feet in back of Stony Creek. Just as had occurred earlier when the flood struck the mountain near South Fork, the impact divided the wave and created a furious backwash. This time, however, the consequences were much graver. One part of the wave, carrying all manner of debris, sped off to the south, rushing up Stony Creek and sweeping over the densely populated suburbs of Kernville and Moxham some three miles away. Then the rising grade forced the water to reverse direction and fall back down toward Johnstown. It met the current coming from the Little Conemaugh, was again swept toward the mountain, and formed a vicious whirlpool. All kinds of debris were caught up in this swirl, including dozens of rooftops to which people clung with the frantic hope of riding out the current. Some of the debris was deposited over Kernville and other parts of the valley to the south. But most was carried to the north, where the other part of the great wave had gone after first striking the side of Westmont Hill—toward the Point where the Little Conemaugh and Stony Creek met to form the Conemaugh—toward the great stone bridge of the Pennsylvania Railroad.

The stone bridge, built to carry four tracks of the railroad across the Conemaugh, was fifty feet wide on top, rose thirty-two feet above the water line, and had seven arches, each fifty-eight feet across. Massive though it was, the bridge would have yielded, like everything else, had the force of the flood struck it fully. Instead, the mountainside caught the brunt of the blow and the bridge had to withstand only a part of the wave. The bridge held firm.

At the Point and the stone bridge all the waters converged, seeking the only way out of the mountains—down the Conemaugh and through the great Conemaugh Gap. Debris quickly built up at the stone arches of the bridge until another impenetrable dam held back the raging waters. Lake Conemaugh formed again, covering the city with nineteen feet of filthy water. For twenty minutes the rising water rammed the earthen embankment at the approach to the bridge until it finally tore out a channel three-hundred feet long and twenty-five feet deep. The flood waters rushed through, striking brutal blows to Millville and Cambria City. The Lincoln Bridge connecting Millville to Johns-

---

"It came like a thief, and was upon us before we were aware. Already when it reached us it had numbered its victims by the hundreds. Mineral Point and East Conemaugh were gone, a passenger train was engulfed. Woodvale was swept away. Conemaugh Borough was shaved off as if by the sharp surface of an avalanche; in a moment Johnstown was tumbling all over itself; houses at one end nodded to houses at the other end and went like a swift, deceitful friend to meet, embrace, and crush them. Then on sped the wreck in a whirl, the angry water baffled for a moment, running up the hill with the town and the helpless multitude on its back, the flood shaking with rage, and dropping here and there a portion of its burden—crushing, grinding, pulverizing all. Then back with the great frame buildings, floating along like ocean steamers, upper decks crowded, hands clinging to every support that could be reached, and so on down to the great stone bridge, where the houses, piled mountain high, took fire, and burned with all the fury of hell you read about. . . ." [*Johnstown Tribune*, June 14, 1889]

COKE OVENS
CONEMAUGH R.
Cambria Iron Works
PENNSYLVANIA RAILROAD
TANNERY
LITTLE CONEMAUGH
Depot
WASHINGTON
CONEMAUGH
LOCUST
MAIN STREET
POINT
UNION
FRANKLIN
CLINTON
JACKSON
ADAM
JOHNSTOWN
LINCOLN
WALNUT
VINE
MARKET
BEDFORD
CHESTNUT
STONY
CREEK
WATER
SOMERSET
HAYNES
DIBERT
MORRIS
NAPOLEON
SHERMAN
SOUTH
B & O RAILROAD
SPRUCE
CHERRY
N

town was destroyed, along with much of the Cambria Company mills. In Cambria City 148 houses were swept away, adding to the countless floating fragments, many carrying human beings—dead and alive—into the lower valley.

Beyond Cambria, the waters spread out and lost their venom. As the flood continued down the Conemaugh it caused little more damage; but the wreckage and corpses deposited as far as the Ohio River gave grim testimony to the havoc it had wrought.

For Johnstown, the nightmare was far from over. Most of the wreckage from the sweep of the valley was jammed into an immense spoilage behind the stone bridge. Wave after wave deposited loads of timber, building fragments, box cars, tangled masses of barbed wire, twisted rails, boulders and rubble, animals and people, until debris stood fifteen feet higher than the top of the bridge. The wreckage formed a nearly watertight mass thirty feet deep, covering over thirty acres from the Point to Main Street.

A little before 6:00 P.M., the drift at the stone bridge caught fire. It began near the eastern end, starting at several places almost simultaneously—perhaps live coals spilled from a stove, or a carload of lime slaked with water ignited. Oil from derailed tank cars fueled the flames. The fire at the drift continued to burn steadily for three days. Those who survived the flames that first night were

---

The raging front wall of water struck Westmont Hill full on, creating a destructive backwash and slamming debris against the great stone bridge. "In it, packed by the force of millions of tons of water moving at nearly 60 miles an hour, were all the trees met by the flood, earth and stone, pieces of bridges, rails and ties, machinery, cars and engine tenders, telegraph poles, miles of wire wrapped round and round whatever it had encountered, pig iron, bricks, boilers, all the spoils of a manufacturing city, all the furniture of innumerable houses, all the contents of innumerable stores and warehouses, all the filth of seven towns, all the animals, and almost all the men and women that lived in them." [John Bach McMaster, *Pennsylvania Magazine of History and Technology,* July 1933.]

Thirty acres of smoldering, water-soaked rubble were bound together by 200,000 pounds of steel wire, immovable and impenetrable by anything but explosives.

rescued on Saturday; but for an unknown number of people trapped inside the debris, the jam at the bridge became an immense funeral pyre.

At nightfall the burning debris cast an eerie glow over the devastated city. For the survivors it was a long, agonizing night. Some crowded into attics or the remains of buildings that somehow had been spared. Alma Hall, a four-story brick office building on Main Street across from the park, had over 260 people in the rooms and hallways that night. Nearly 200 people were in the upper floors of the Union Street School; another 175 found shelter at the Morrell Institute. Close to 90 people crammed into a brick house at the corner of Vine and Stony Creek streets, and another house on Vine had 51 people in the attic. Fearful of natural gas leaks, they did not dare strike a light. And so they huddled in darkness—except for the lurid glow of the burning debris. Buildings collapsed all around, unable to withstand any longer the pressure of the debris and the water, which still flowed as deep as twenty feet. With each grinding and creaking of a floorboard, the frightened people inside must have wondered whether their refuge would be the next to fall. For others clinging to slippery rooftops or branches of trees, with water lapping at their heels and rain still pelting them from above, the night must have seemed endless.

Everyone had terrifying memories of what had happened: the awful mist; the great rush of the water; the shudder and collapse of buildings among shattered glass and crumbling plaster; the desperate grab for a piece of wreckage to keep afloat; the struggle to catch a loved one from being pulled under by the current; the careening, whirling ride through the rushing waters, crashing and grabbing again, resuming the horrifying ride, or hitting the jam, or being one of the lucky few rescued. Nearly everyone saw friends, neighbors, or relatives disappear to certain death, or presumed the worst about missing loved ones. And now, for the survivors there were the screams for help, the groans of the wounded, the cries of frightened children, the crashing of buildings, the crackling of fires, the interminable splashing of water, the creaking of shifting wreckage, and through it all the knell of the town clock. Miraculously, the clock mechanism had survived in the steeple of the German Lutheran Church on Jackson Street, and it continued to sound the hours. The unforgettable sounds of that long night told all that the ordeal had been no garish dream, no fiendish nightmare from which they would soon awaken.

The thousands of people who witnessed the ravaging of Johnstown from the hillsides—many having reached safe ground with only seconds to spare—also knew this had been no dream. With the first streaks of light they began to gather on the fringes of Green Hill, Prospect Hill, and other slopes, straining their eyes to see. The rain had finally stopped, but across the valley below hung a low shroud of mist and smoke.

They began to make out a few familiar shapes—the Methodist Church, Alma Hall, Union Street School, the schoolhouse on Adams Street, the Wood, Morrell and Company Store, and Cambria Company's general offices were all in place. But elsewhere they saw only huge piles of rubbish and vast vacant tracts of mud. Where yesterday the houses and businesses were as thick as they could be built, there was now nothing but open space, mud, and scattered wreckage. Washington Street was swept clean except for the B&O Station. The four-story Hulbert House was gone; it had collapsed the instant the flood wave hit, killing forty-eight of the sixty people who had sought safety in the substantial-looking new hotel. A cluster of commercial buildings remained on Main, but the wreckage around them almost reached to the rooftops. Looking up the Stony Creek,

Looking toward Woodvale, across the sheared valley where the Gautier Mills and Conemaugh Borough once stood. "Through Conemaugh Borough joining the lower end of Woodvale and stretching away southward, the waters cut a clean swath. . . . Brick buildings were shaved off to the earth's surface, and frames jammed into an indistinguishable mass of ruin. Roland's feed-store, a two-story brick, withstood and helped divide the torrent. A moving rampart, bristling with the spoils gathered on its remorseless way, mowed down Railroad, Jackson, Feeder, Clinton and Bedford streets clear to Stony Creek. . . . Blocks of buildings smashed against each other, the swishing foe rending them asunder to augment the fearful burden of a wasted district." [J. J. McLaurin]

B.&O. PASSENGER STATION

Kernville was unrecognizable—virtually everything was gone. Looking to the Point, the entire western end of Johnstown was a mountain of burning debris. The ironworks below the stone bridge were still standing, but badly damaged. Cambria City, further downstream, was buried under a pile of muck and rock, and two-thirds of its houses had disappeared.

"Well, the reservoir came, and Johnstown went visiting. Some of us on very long visits indeed—never to come back. All that is left to most of us is the ground the town was built on, and even that is not the same." [*Johnstown Tribune*, June 14, 1889]

Top, left to right
A panorama of Johnstown, after much of the debris had been cleared away. Stony Creek is in the foreground. The Cambria Mills, back in operation, and the stone bridge are in the background at left. Company houses line up on Prospect Hill. Green Hill, where thousands of survivors found refuge, is right of the gap. Kernville, heavily damaged from the backwash of Stony Creek, is at the right.

"As . . . we gazed back upon our city, or where our city was, our hearts sank within us. To the right stood the blackened walls of St. John's Roman Catholic Church. Here and there above . . . the massed piles of bricks . . . were a few houses standing, some of them out of plumb. The spires of churches once our pride were gone; the most of our homes, destroyed, and their fragments scattered over the wide vale below. It were vain to undertake to tell the world how or what we felt, when shoeless, hatless, and many of us almost naked, some bruised and broken, we stood there and looked upon that scene of death and desolation." [The Reverend D. J. Beale]

Bottom, left to right
Fire destroyed much of what the flood had left standing. Here, the remains of St. John's.

The B & O passenger station at Washington and Franklin, formerly Johnstown's first high school building, miraculously survived the flood and served as a morgue.

The Wood, Morrell and Company Store and adjacent general offices of the Cambria Iron Company were among the few buildings left standing on Washington Street.

As people moved down from the hillsides, they could see the shapes of other survivors coming out of the buildings that had harbored them through the night and picking their way gingerly across the flotsam. The closer everyone looked, the more hopeless and heartbreaking the desolation appeared. The stunned survivors moved over acres of debris searching for some trace of their homes or even of the streets where they had stood. Everywhere were scattered the reminders of thousands of lives: broken dishes, toys, quilts, furniture, bicycle wheels, Bibles. Everywhere gutted houses had spilled their contents. And everywhere human corpses, strewn in all manner of grotesque conditions and shapes, populated the ghastly scene.

Numb with shock and hunger and cold, the survivors somehow managed to collect their senses. They faced immediate and critical problems. Thousands of people were homeless; hundreds injured. There was no medicine, no dry clothing, no water fit to drink, no food to eat. Nearly all the stores in town had been destroyed, along with their stocks. Saturday would have been market day for the housewives in the boroughs, so even where houses had been spared, the cupboards were nearly bare. There

---

Facing page
"At the foot of Washington street, Walnut ran at right angles. No sign of it anywhere. The iron bridge to the Pennsylvania railroad and the wooden one behind the store have strayed off, and men across the stream are beginning to set rows of bodies on the station platform. The water keeps them and us apart." [J. J. McLaurin]

"From Franklin street Locust is a remembrance only, its dwellings in flinders and ridges of sand concealing its surface." [J. J. McLaurin]

Right
Residents of Kernville were victims of heavy destruction when the backwash from Westmont Hill and the stone bridge swept up Stony Creek.

"Twenty-five families [in Cambria City] left no surviving member to say what had become of them, and over half the town was stripped bare as a hungry dog could scrape a bone." [J. J. McLaurin]

was no gas or electricity. Fires burned out of control in several places. Communication with the outside world seemed impossible. Every telegraph and telephone line was down; roads were impassable; the railroad was destroyed; bridges were gone. Corpses of the flood's victims—not only human beings, but horses, farm animals, dogs, cats, chickens, birds, rats—presented a real threat of disease.

Yet in the midst of this chaos, reason prevailed. Rescue parties were already at work pulling the injured and marooned from rooftops, trees, attics, and from the burning wreckage at the bridge. All morning long, farmers came down from the hillsides with wagons of food, water and dry clothing. Milk was passed out by the tinful to hungry children. By mid-afternoon, showing extraordinary calm, every man who could get there met at the Adams Street School to discuss what to do. They elected Arthur J. Moxham as "dictator" to take charge of the recovery effort. Moxham immediately organized citizens' committees for setting up temporary hospitals and morgues; for removal of the dead; for distribution of local supplies; for information, transportation, registration, sanitation, police, etc. Methodically the people of Johnstown went about their tasks, seemingly grateful to have some purpose assigned to their lives so they would not have to think too much about what had happened.

"Everything about us was in inextricable confusion, showing the effects of the terrific convulsion through which nature and humanity had passed. Here were uprooted trees, houses upturned or demolished, furniture of every description—hardware, woodenware, parlor ornaments and kitchen utensils, mattresses, bodies of horses, cattle and swine, corpses of men, women, and children, railroad cars and locomotives—overturned or on end, and pressing down upon the half-buried bodies of the drowned." [The Reverend David J. Beale]

Far left, bottom
People claimed a "miracle" occurred in St. Mary's Roman Catholic Church in Cambria City because a statue of the Virgin Mary was not damaged by the flood. Made of wood, the statue was light enough to float while the heavier pedestal kept it upright, and when the waters receded, statue and pedestal returned to their proper place.

"Where is Washington street, the first paralleling Conemaugh Creek? Between it and the stream were the Baltimore & Ohio tracks and yards, sheds and freight houses, a hotel or two, the opera-house and the big store. Everything else is blank space. . . . Not a particle of its seventy or eighty saloons, its stores, shops, restaurants and dwellings is to be seen. The buildings and their contents swell the drift and refuse that gorge Kernville or sustain the blaze on the Point, while the cellars are packed with mud and stones and dead bodies. Two hundred persons were in these three blocks when the deluge hit them." [J. J. McLaurin]

"Locust street, a square back of Washington is the next in order. The upper part is planted with wrecks, yet a fair percentage of its own buildings did not flit. . . . The snug brick residences in rear of the Methodist Church were roughly handled—bay windows absent, porches not at their posts, the furniture coated with slime and the inmates scattered." [J. J. McLaurin]

Main and Central Park with Dr. Lowman's house in the background. "This brings us to the Park, which a jaunty fence had enclosed. Grass and trees flanked the cinder paths, and thousands crossed the plot daily. Look at it! The trees, the fence, the grass, the paths have made room for a Babel of confusion." [J. J. McLaurin]

From the hill behind the Adams Street schoolhouse morgue toward what had been Main and Bedford streets. "Swank's brick block—four stories filled with hardware and agricultural implements—stood on this spot, the southeast corner of Main and Bedford streets. A two-story brick was mortised in the north end where the streets form an acute angle. A grocery occupied the ground floor and the *Herald* was printed upstairs. The cylinder of the printing press lies in the cellar across the way, and the roof of the Swank block is distributed over the site of Hon. Daniel McLaughlin's mansion." [J. J. McLaurin]

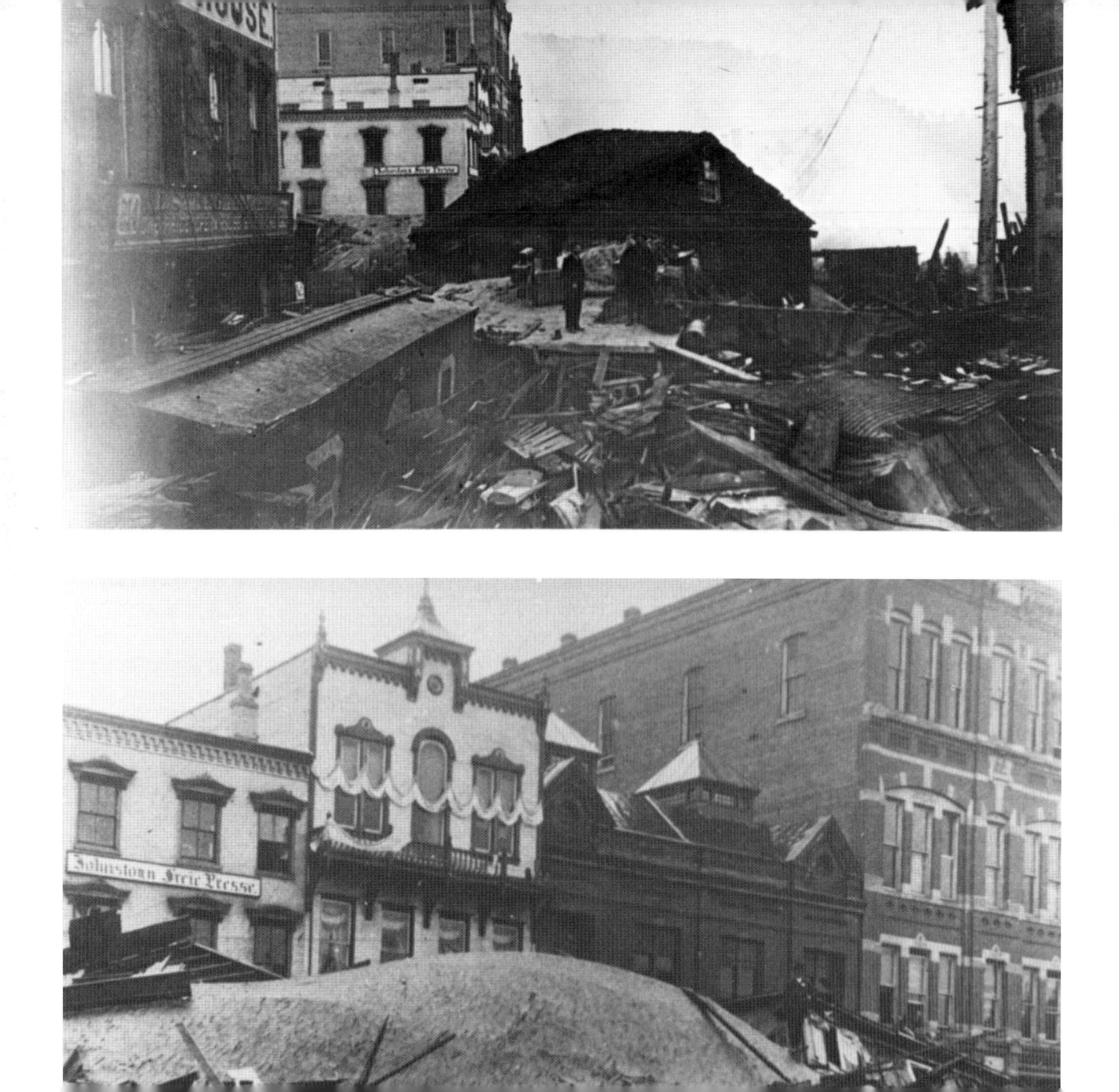
HOUSE.
Johnstown Freie Presse

Facing page, top to bottom
Main Street, looking west. "A box-car holds the fort in the middle of the street, and a weather-beaten house reinforces it. The car is labelled 'B&O' which settles its identity, but none can recognize the tenement." [J. J. McLaurin]

The Memorial Day bunting still clings to buildings on Main Street. "This is Alma Hall [building to right] four stories in height, a store and a gas-office below, law offices and lodge rooms higher up. The flood washed swarms of people toward the hall, where they were rescued. Three hundred found refuge within it all night, some coming over mountains of obstructions at the peril of life and limb." [J. J. McLaurin]

Above, left to right
"Clinton street—passing down Main we glanced at it—presents fresh surprises. From Washington to Main it was built up principally with stores, hotels and shops, families occupying the upper floors. Three doors from Main, on the east side of the street, mark the basement filled with muck and wreckage. On this spot stood the Hulbert House, the leading hostelry. . . . The great wave crushed buildings and streets, opened a broad lane and tilted against the wing of the hotel. The result was astounding. The whole building reeled, parted, disappeared! Fifty lives went out in the bewildering crash." [J. J. McLaurin]

". . . great slices of wreck pitched headlong into the yard of the Cambria Iron Works. The upper end of the rail mill was torn out. Boilers wriggled from their brick arches and engines executed strange gyrations. Stones and earth showered acres of the yard to the depth of ten or twelve feet, covering a train of freight cars. . . . Fifteen persons were thrown upon the roof of the rail mill to be swept off the next instant by a whirling mass of timbers." [J. J. McLaurin]

Above, left to right

From Clinton Street, looking east on Main Street. "The Merchants' Hotel, a four-story brick, vibrates in the breeze. Part of the rear was thrown down, taking with it a porch and two guests. The next building is past redemption, and Luckhardt's frame is so racked and twisted that it must be pulled down." [J. J. McLaurin]

Wreckage piled two and three stories high on Main Street. "A hundred people spent last night on the roof of John Thomas's building, which defied the incursions of the flood. The wreckage is twenty-five feet deep, with a thickening tendency. . . . How many human bodies we have stepped on and over cannot be guessed." [J. J. McLaurin]

Facing page, top to bottom

Editor Swank chronicled the events of the flood from this building. "Soon we reach the corner of Main and Franklin. . . . The opera-house is bunched in the jam. It sailed from Washington street, by what route nobody can tell, and is touching the building used as the Bijou opera-house for years. Queer, isn't it, that the two should cuddle together at last? . . . The *Tribune* office, in the second story, had a bit of side-wall hustled out, type pied and presses hurt." [J. J. McLaurin]

"The Park begins at the northwest corner, and Frazier's drug-store faces it on the northeast. The building is considerably the worse of the tussle, a good piece of one wall falling in the affray." [J. J. McLaurin]

Left
"Once more we enter Adams street. Groups loiter on the sidewalks. . . . Listen: 'Good-day,' says one, 'how many lost?' 'Six' is the brief reply, spoken as coldly as if the weather were the topic. . . . 'I wonder if my daughter is found,' asks an old woman, as six men pass with a body on a stretcher. They place it in the schoolhouse, which is to be the morgue." [J. J. McLaurin]

Corpses were washed—first with hoses or buckets of water to remove the mud, then more carefully. Clothing was cut off and the bodies embalmed and wrapped in muslin. Here at the Fourth Ward morgue, at the Adams Street school, a body is being lifted through a window to be placed in the coffin below. People witnessed so much death and horror that they became calloused to such sights. Several chroniclers noted that the survivors of the flood showed little evidence of their grief, as though their emotions had dammed up until they could not even weep.

Facing page, top
Dr. D. J. Beale (standing, left), pastor of the Presbyterian Church, surveys the damage in Central Park. His church is at right; the Presbyterian parsonage is behind it; the Disciples' Church is center; and Alma Hall is at left.

Bottom
Coffins were brought in by the carload. "The coffins were stacked around the morgues, on the pavements and at the railway stations. They were the first thing to greet the stranger and send a frigid current down the spine of the visitor. Many were small as violin cases—for the great army of babies and young children. The heaps lessened steadily, for bodies were dug out daily for five months." [J. J. McLaurin]

Facing page, top, left to right
The observation tower at Sang Hollow was as close as Superintendent Pitcairn could get to Johnstown on the day of the flood; but he learned enough here to spread news of the devastation.

General D. H. Hastings and 580 men of the 14th Regiment from Pittsburgh made camp in the center of the city to keep order and carry out the relief work. Alma Hall is at the right of this photograph, and the Franklin Street Methodist Church is at center.

Facing page, bottom, left to right
Central Park was cleared of ten- to fifteen-foot piles of debris in four days to make room for the militia camp.

Sentries were posted to keep out sightseers and troublemakers. This military post at Kernville overlooked the center of Johnstown.

"The crowds around the commissaries . . . are a mud-bedraggled set. The entrance to each [relief] station is very narrow; yet into them the women and children, each with a capacious basket, crowd like sheep in a pen. . . . The baskets are generally well filled, yet on leaving the commissaries, complaints are heard on all sides of 'No butter, nor anything fresh after two weeks.' " [New York *Evening Post*, June 14, 1889]

Right, top
A survivor signs up for rations at the state militia camp in the center of Johnstown.

Right, bottom
The relief station at the Pennsylvania Railroad Station.

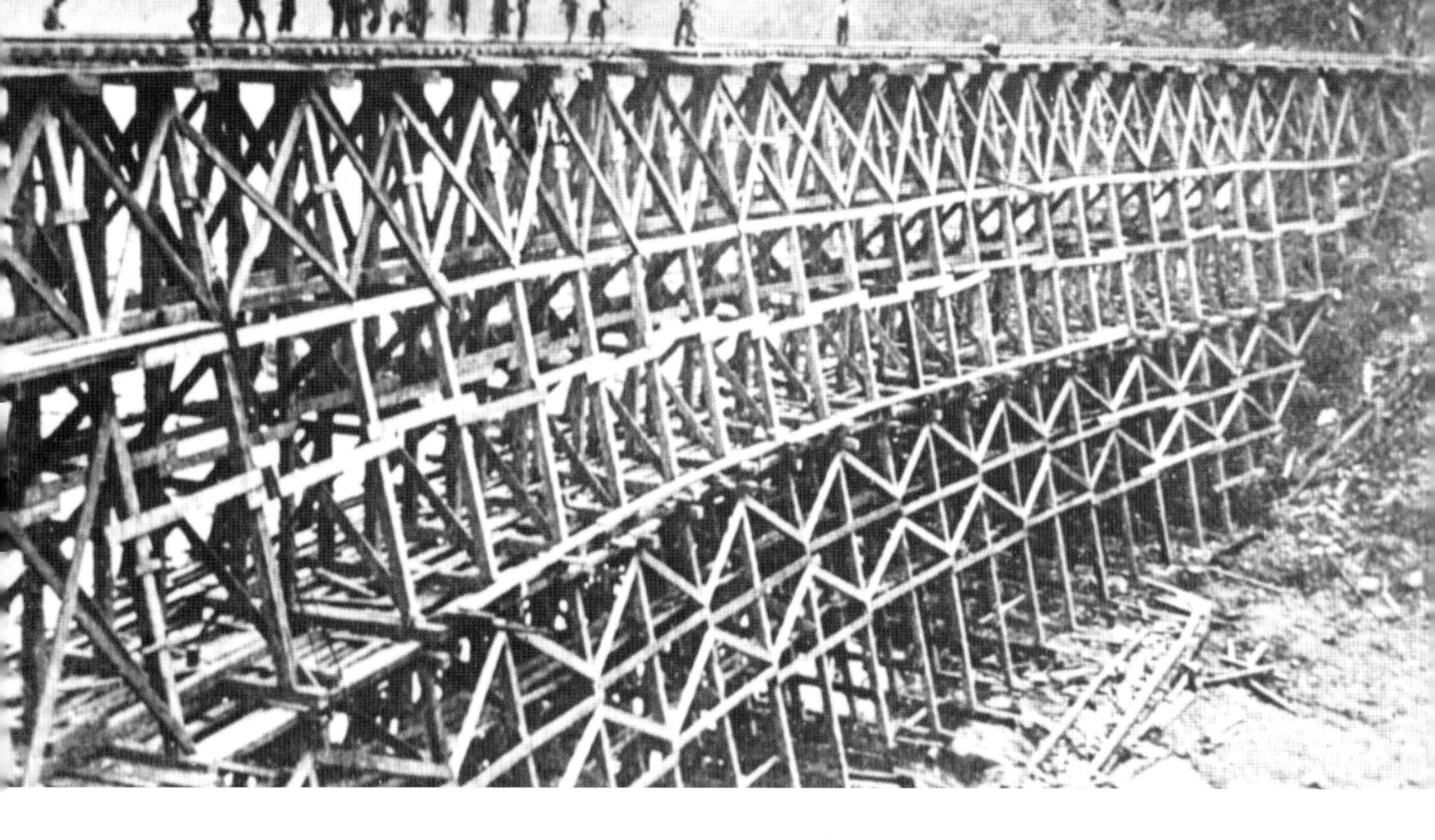

Meanwhile, word of the catastrophe reached the outside world. Ironically, a member of the South Fork Fishing and Hunting Club, Robert Pitcairn, was the first to spread the news. Pitcairn, superintendent of the Pennsylvania Railroad's Pittsburgh Division, had been heading east on Friday to check on reported landslides, but his train could get only as far as Sang Hollow, a few miles below Johnstown. From the dead and living who floated down the swollen Conemaugh, Pitcairn surmised what had happened. He telegraphed a message to the *Pittsburgh Commercial Gazette* saying that Johnstown had been annihilated and that relief was needed immediately. Pitcairn then headed back to Pittsburgh to help organize relief efforts.

Pitcairn's first message from Sang Hollow reached Pittsburgh about 7:00 P.M. on Friday. By the time he sent a more detailed message from New Florence, the *Gazette* had already chartered a special train to take its reporters to the scene of the disaster.

This first trainload of newsmen left Pittsburgh at 11:00 P.M. Friday. When they could travel no further by train, they went overland by horse and buggy, then by foot all through the night. By dawn Saturday, June 1, a weary group of reporters stood among the people on the hillsides above Johnstown, staring in disbelief at the wasteland below.

These reporters were only the first of many to come. Not since the assassination of Abraham Lincoln had there been a news story like this. Within the first few days after the flood, more than a hundred reporters converged on Johnstown from all parts of the country. Along with them came telegraph operators, magazine editors, authors, artists, and an estimated two hundred photographers. They described and photographed the disaster from every conceivable angle. Newsmen vied in friendly rivalry to outdo one another's stories. In the confusion of the first days after the flood, and later in their enthusiasm for headlines, the reporters often blurred or exaggerated the facts and added extra melodrama to a story that needed no embellishment. Yet no matter how much they wrote, nor how florid their descriptions, the appetites of their readers for news were unsatiated. One Pittsburgh newspaper sold so many extra copies in the days following the calamity that it had to reduce the size of the pages until it could obtain more paper.

The Great Flood of 1889 was the epitome of horror for the Victorian Age. The greatest natural disaster of the century, it touched the emotions of all levels of society. The rush of the waters on unsuspecting Johnstown, the violation of happy homes, the cruel drownings and horrors at the bridge, the plight of orphans and widows, the recovery of the dead—all these became subjects of conversation, poetry, novels, legends, and song. However incredible the descriptions coming from Johnstown may have sounded, the photographs soon showed gruesome evidence that the calamity was real.

The newspaper accounts aroused sympathies of people throughout the nation and the world and resulted in a lavish outpouring of charity. Less than twenty-four hours after the disaster, the first organized relief began at Pittsburgh, where Robert Pitcairn addressed a meeting in the old city hall. His descriptions, together with reports coming in from towns down river from Johnstown, left no doubt of the need for immediate and generous help. Two men stood outside the hall after the meeting and collected $48,116.70 in less than an hour.

From the outset, Pittsburgh was the leading contributor to Johnstown's relief. As the nearest large city to the stricken area, it served as a custodian for relief money and a clearinghouse for supplies that soon poured in for Johnstown. Pittsburgh and vicinity raised over $250,000 and received over $800,000 from other areas. Philadelphia, Harrisburg, and New York also served

Railroads throughout the valley were devastated by the flood and had to be rebuilt quickly to open the way for food and supplies. Working around the clock, crews restored regular traffic within two weeks of the flood. This wooden trestle, 80 feet high and 400 feet long, was constructed in just five days to replace the old stone viaduct which the flood had destroyed.

as major collecting points. In all, more than $3,000,000 was donated for the Johnstown cause. The money came from all over: Boston gave $94,000; Chicago collected $70,500; Kansas City gave $12,000. The state of Connecticut gave $25,000. Various fraternal organizations and lodges contributed $260,000. Wealthy individuals gave: Andrew Carnegie, $5,000; John Jacob Astor, $2,500; Joseph Pulitzer, $2,000; Jay Gould, $1,000. Businesses gave: Westinghouse, $15,000; the New York Stock Exchange, $20,000; the Pennsylvania Railroad, $5,000; Macy's, $1,000. Churches took up special collections. Theatres and orchestras held benefits. School children sent in nickels and dimes. Sixteen foreign countries sent a total of $141,300, including contributions from the Sultan of Turkey and the Lord Mayor of Dublin.

In addition to the money, gifts of food and clothing came from throughout the country: Cleveland sent twenty-eight carloads of lumber; Minneapolis sent sixteen carloads of flour; Cincinnati sent 20,000 pounds of ham. The prisoners of Pennsylvania's Western Penitentiary baked 1,000 loaves of bread a day for Johnstown. Other cities and individuals contributed coffins, embalming fluid, blankets, mattresses, soap, nails, medicine, and so on. Still others contributed their services as undertakers, physicians, and laborers. The railroads gave free passage to all supplies donated to the relief effort and to survivors of the flood who wanted to leave the stricken city.

Johnstown and the surrounding boroughs needed all the charity that was offered. Not only were there more than 28,000 survivors, but also more than 6,000 relief workers and newcomers to be fed each day. Some 15,000 people had to be clothed and housed. Thousands of human bodies and animal carcasses had to be found and disposed of; acres of wreckage had to be cleared; water and utilities had to be restored; and now trainloads of provisions and great amounts of cash had to be distributed.

That all of this was accomplished in orderly fashion is a credit to many participants: the local relief committees; the Pittsburgh Relief Corps, which took charge from June 4 until June 12; the state militia, which took over on June 12 under the command of Adjutant-General Daniel Hartman Hastings; and the American Red Cross, under the direction of Clara Barton.

Miss Barton, a resolute sixty-seven-year-old spinster, stood only five feet tall in her stocking feet, but she commanded the respect and obedience of everyone around her. She had served humanity through the Civil War and the Franco-Prussian War, and in 1881 she had succeeded in establishing an American Branch of the International Red Cross. Johnstown was the first major disaster for the infant organization, and Clara Barton intended to prove its worth in just such emergencies. When she arrived from Washington, D.C., on June 5 with a group of men and women from the American Red Cross, Clara Barton announced they were there to stay as long as needed.

Her work kept her in Johnstown for five months. During that time she and her people worked tirelessly to distribute the supplies arriving daily by the train load; to supervise construction of several "Red Cross Hotels" for temporary housing, a large warehouse, and an infirmary; and to direct hundreds of volunteers in the relief effort. The Philadelphia Chapter of the Red Cross also served Johnstown well, setting up an efficient medical and surgical service, first in a hospital tent at Wood and Cedar streets, and then in the Cambria Iron Company's hospital on Prospect Hill. Before leaving Johnstown, the Philadelphia unit organized what became the Conemaugh Valley Memorial Hospital.

While the Red Cross coordinated the relief effort, the state took charge of the massive cleanup effort. Fear for the public health, not only for survivors of the flood, but also for the many other communities which drew water supplies from the Conemaugh, led the governor of Pennsylvania to call out the state militia. He put General Hastings in charge of operations at Johnstown. Under Hastings' able command, the militia kept order in the city, guarded the growing number of supplies, established and monitored a commissary system, kept sightseers and relic hunters out of the way, and supervised the nearly 6,000 laborers who came from all over to work on the cleanup.

Sanitation was a critical concern. Each day the sun grew warmer, hastening decomposition of remaining bodies and animal carcasses. The water flowing under the debris at the bridge and on down the river became foul. Standing water in great mudholes everywhere became more polluted. The state Board of Health quickly organized a sanitary corps to cremate animal carcasses, to clean out cellars clogged with all manner of filth, and to disinfect everything. People in the valley were given disinfectants and taught how to use them. In the Kernville section alone, twelve wagonloads of disinfectants were spread daily. The 222 laborers and twenty-two inspectors in the Sanitary Corps worked so efficiently that there was only one outbreak of infectious disease. Between June 10 and July 25, 461 people contracted typhoid fever, of which forty died.

The Red Cross built several "hotels" to provide temporary housing for the afflicted. "To meet these necessities, and being apprehensive that some good lives might go out under the existing lack of accommodation, it was decided to erect a building similar to our warehouse. The use of the former site of the Episcopal Church was generously tendered us. . . . This house, which was soon erected, was known as the 'Locust Street Red Cross Hotel'; it was fifty by one hundred and sixteen feet in dimensions, two stories in height, with lantern roof, built of hemlock, single siding, papered inside with heavy building paper, and heated by natural gas, as all our buildings were. It consisted of thirty-four rooms, besides kitchen, laundry, bath rooms with hot and cold water, and one main dining-hall and sitting room through the centre, sixteen feet in width by one hundred in length with second floor gallery." [Clara Barton]

The dining room of Red Cross Hotel No. 3. "A competent landlady, who like the rest, had a few weeks before floated down over that same ground on the roof of her house in thirty feet of water five miles below the city, rescued in a tree top, was placed in charge, with instructions to keep a good house, make what she could, rent free, but charging no Johnstown person over twenty-five cents for a meal of food." [Clara Barton]

Left
Some of the relics that the flood left in Cambria City. The Cambria Iron Works are in the background.

Despite damage to the east end of the main building of the mill, the Cambria Iron Works resumed operation by June 24, reassuring citizens that Johnstown could rebuild.

Facing page, top, left to right
Arthur Kirk of Pittsburgh was an explosives expert. Reporters looking for stories found the "Prince of Dynamiters" good copy. "He personally superintends the preparation of all blasts, and when ready emits a peculiar cry, more like a wail than a warning. Then he surveys the atmosphere with the air of a major general and yells 'Fire!' The yell often terrifies the spectators more than the explosion." [Richard O'Connor]

"Dynamite added its horror to the mass of wreckage that lies above the railroad bridge. A half dozen times this afternoon the heavy thunder of the huge cartridges was heard for miles around and fragments of the debris flew high in the air while at a distance the crowd looked on in dreadful sorrow. . . ." [A New York *Sun* reporter, quoted in Richard O'Connor]

Facing page, bottom, left to right
Telegraph communications resumed within twenty-four hours of the flood. News stories poured out of Johnstown to the Associated Press and the great metropolitan daily papers. More than one hundred reporters came to cover the story, working out of crude headquarters in a brick kiln. They played an important role. "Correspondents for the great papers pictured the scenes in such graphic pen portraiture that almost before the maddened waters subsided the great heart of the mighty nation had been touched with sympathy, and pocketbooks and checkbooks made quick response to the city for help and succor." [New York *Daily Graphic*, June 13, 1889]

The flood wiped out nearly all bridges joining parts of the city and the boroughs. Temporary bridges were quickly installed to restore communication and transport supplies.

AYERS

The mass of debris at the stone bridge presented the most difficult single problem for the cleanup crews. Nothing would move the more than thirty acres of tightly woven, charred, water-soaked ruins. A demolition expert from Pittsburgh, Arthur Kirk, known as the "Prince of Dynamiters," took on the task. Using 1,000 pounds of explosives donated by the Dynamite Company of New York, Kirk set off his first blasts on June 5. People could not help thinking about the remains of hundreds of bodies still buried in the mass as fragments of debris were blasted into the air.

Even Kirk had trouble breaking up the jam. By June 10 he had succeeded in clearing an area only 100 × 300 feet. Steam winches were set up on the bridge to try to break apart what the explosives loosened. A crew of 200 lumberjacks from Michigan attacked the wire-bound wreckage with their axes, but nothing seemed to penetrate it.

Kirk increased the amount of explosives until citizens feared he would knock down what the flood had left standing. He set off a 450-pound charge that broke windows and cracked plaster for miles. Kirk finally yielded to public protests and agreed to use smaller charges and to confine the blasting to daytime. At night, Kirk's men set fire to sections of the drift. This was quieter, perhaps, but nonetheless disruptive to sleep for the beleaguered citizens. The blasting and burning continued until

---

By mid-summer, most merchants were back in business. General Hastings had arranged for the makers of the "Hughes" houses to build temporary frame buildings around the four sides of Central Park. Business and professional men drew lots for the stores and offices.

Relief officials encouraged women and children to leave the devastated area during the cleanup, and the railroads offered free passage to any flood victims who had friends or relatives to shelter them, no matter how distant. But most stayed to help, taking housing where they could.

August 22, nearly three months after the flood, when at last the drift was cleared away and the two mountain streams could again flow freely into the Conemaugh.

The search for bodies continued for months. As late as October 26, bodies were found between Johnstown and Nineveh, seven miles downstream. Over a hundred morticians, who were among the first volunteers to reach Johnstown after the flood, worked almost around the clock to clean, embalm, register, and wrap the bodies in shrouds for burial. Usually only the briefest descriptions could be written in the morgue records: ". . . 25. Unknown, Female. Light hair. About fifteen years." The bodies were laid out at various temporary morgues for the crowds of people who were searching for some familiar face or form. At first, bodies not immediately identified were kept two days before interment. But as the decomposition advanced, the bodies had to be buried without delay. Six hundred forty-three of the 1,491 bodies recovered by June 11 remained unidentified.

There never would be a precise count of the casualties. The number generally accepted as the total dead is 2,209. One out of three bodies found was never identified; 967 persons were listed as "not known to be found." Of the dead, 396 were children ten years or younger. The flood left 98 orphans, 124 widows, and 198 widowers. One of the most telling statistics of the Great

Laborers lined up for payday. Above average wages for the time—two dollars per day plus room and board—attracted more than six thousand men to the valley. Teamsters came from as far as Ohio and New York for the five dollars a day a man with a team could secure.

Prefabricated houses were brought in to help the critical housing shortage. The "Oklahomas," one-room 10 × 20 foot cottages, and the slightly larger "Ready Mades," proved too small for family living. Relief officials contracted with a Chicago firm for some four hundred two-story, four-room "Hughes" houses. The one- and two-story Oklahomas are shown in the center of this photograph, flanked by two of the larger Hughes houses.

M. J. KENNEDY.
HARD & SOFT COAL

Flood of 1889 is that 99 families, with two to ten members, were completely annihilated.

As the statistics of death and property losses mounted, public bitterness against the members of the South Fork Fishing and Hunting Club also increased. Newspapers throughout the nation denounced the sportsmen and their playground. Few people doubted the club's culpability in the failure of the dam. A New York *World* reporter quoted General Hastings saying: "It was a piece of carelessness, I might say criminal negligence." Editor Swank spoke for all Johnstowners when he wrote in the first edition of the *Tribune* to follow the flood: "We think we know what struck us, and it was not the hand of Providence. Our misery is the work of man. . . ."

A coroner's jury from Westmoreland County investigating the cause of death of 121 bodies pulled from the Conemaugh at Nine-

---

Far left, top
People became accustomed to hearing "Hold it," as photographers asked their subjects to pose for the cameras, as here, in front of the Adams Street schoolhouse morgue.

Far left, bottom
Sightseers and relic hunters flocked to Johnstown. As early as June 16, 1889, the B&O Railroad sold an excursion trip to Johnstown for $2.35 roundtrip, allowing tourists four hours in town. The advertisements noted: "Those who desire to go on this excursion should provide themselves with lunch baskets as provisions cannot be procured at Johnstown." Some citizens resented the sightseers; others sold relics to the curious. The site of the South Fork Dam became a popular attraction, as suggested here, and today is a National Park Service site attracting thousands each year.

Left
Sometimes the photographers, like the reporters, embellished the facts. This photograph is probably a fake, with someone posing as a flood victim. By the time the photographers arrived on the scene, a body so well exposed would have been removed.

But for the most part, the cameras recorded the awful truth.

veh issued its verdict on June 7: ". . . death by violence due to the flood caused by the breaking of the dam of the South Fork Reservoir. . . ." The Cambria County coroner's inquest returned a similar conclusion regarding the cause of death of a flood victim: ". . . we find the owners of said dam were culpable in not making it as secure as it should have been, especially in view of the fact that a population of many thousands were in the valley below; and we hold that the owners are responsible for the fearful loss of life and property resulting from the breaking of the dam."

Representatives of the engineering profession conducted investigations and determined that the actions of the South Fork Club had weakened the dam. The engineers noted four primary causes for the dam's failure: the lowering of the crest, the central sag in the crest, the closing of the bottom culvert after which no means of lowering the water level existed, and the obstruction of the spillway. A report by the American Society of Civil Engineers concluded that the "failure was due to flow of water over the top of the earthen embankment, caused by the insufficiency of the wasteway to discharge the flood water."

Public opinion, the coroners' reports, and the engineers' investigations censured the club, but none of the club members was ever held legally accountable. In lawsuits filed against the club for negligence, the jury upheld the sportsmen's claim that the disaster had been a "visitation of Providence." Although many of the club members contributed money to the relief effort, no money was collected for damages from anyone associated with the club. Whether the courts would have ruled differently if the cases had been tried in Johnstown instead of Pittsburgh, or had been tried by today's standards, is open to conjecture.

The pleasures of their idyllic summer retreat were washed away by the waters of Lake Conemaugh, and the club members never returned to South Fork. Their fashionable cottages and clubhouse stood empty along the edges of a vast mud flat. Gone were the boathouses and bath houses that once dotted the shores; gone were the yachts and the sailboats and the boardwalks. Membership declined, notes fell due; and in July 1891 the grounds of the South Fork Fishing and Hunting Club were divided and sold off at a sheriff's sale. Eventually, the village of St. Michael was built on the former lakebed between the South Fork and the club cottages.

Buoyed by the aid and encouragement that came from all directions, the people of Johnstown dug into the task of rebuilding their city and their lives. Recovery began immediately, and the city was soon bustling again—this time with the sounds of dynamite blasts, hammers and saws, wagons and teams, and train after train of relief supplies. In his June 14 editorial in the *Tribune*, George Swank wrote:

> We have today a ruined town of Johnstown and ruined neighbors, but in six months hence we will show that we have an attachment to the places where our hearthstones once rested that cannot be broken, an abiding faith in our town, and above all an interest in each other and a faith in each other, born of the sore affliction which will not suffer us to give up or run away.

His prophecy came true, perhaps even faster than Swank himself could have imagined. By the end of June, temporary bridges were in place; the Wood, Morrell and Company store and a few other stores were open, selling reclaimed goods; and the First National Bank was back in business. By mid-July the Cambria Iron works reopened, and three newspapers were being published again. By fall, temporary stores had been erected on the public square. Merchants could occupy these for as long as eighteen months while they rebuilt their businesses. Prefabricated "Oklahoma" and "Hughes" houses were going up like mushrooms throughout the city. The gas company restored service by October, and by then most homes and businesses had electric lights.

General Hastings and the militia withdrew in July. Most of the state's role in the cleanup was completed by September. The last of the commissaries, which had served 30,000 people a day in June, closed October 5, with only 465 still on the rolls. By the end of October, Clara Barton could say with pride: "Enterprising, industrious and hopeful, the new Johnstown, phoenix-like, rose from its ruins, more beautiful than the old." The American Red Cross then retired from the scene, the last of the relief organizations to leave Johnstown.

The rehabilitation of Johnstown united the populace in a common goal. Before the flood, borough loyalty and jealousy thwarted any efforts toward consolidation. But recovery from the Great Flood made extraordinary demands on local governments, and it was clear that a common government could plan and coordinate the reconstruction better than separate boroughs. The citizens accepted consolidation at the November election, and on December 18, 1889, the charter of the new city of Johnstown was signed by the governor.

It would be many months, several years really, before life returned to normal for the people of the Conemaugh Valley. While the work of cleanup and recovery continued, efforts were already under way to provide an appropriate memorial to the flood's victims. Beginning in August 1889 and continuing through November, bodies of the unknown dead were raised at several cemeteries where they had been hastily buried. They were reinterred in the new Grand View Cemetery, high atop a

For the children who survived, the flood and its aftermath were especially bewildering. But they were lucky; not so, the nearly 400 children under age ten killed in the flood. "Perhaps the saddest feature of the disaster was the dreadful slaughter of the children. . . . the lamentable scarcity of children impressed itself painfully upon every mind. The cries of babies . . . the merry laughter of boys and girls were seldom heard. The lack of animation in the boys . . . was too apparent to pass unheeded. They took no interest in the arrival of the trains, the unloading of provisions, or any of the exciting scenes which the calamity occasioned. The little girls—there were not enough of them to be in anybody's way or to attract the slightest bit of attention. . . . A community bereft of its children is the bitterest evidence of the horrible devastation." [J. J. McLaurin]

Seated on the remains of the old Conemaugh Viaduct, these flood victims appear to be carrying what few possessions they have salvaged.

hill overlooking the valley. The Pennsylvania Flood Relief Commission purchased 20,000 square feet for the reburial plot. With the hope that more corpses would be identified in the transfer, the remains were again laid out for public viewing. A total of 844 bodies were raised, of which 76 were known; 34 others were identified in the transfer. The 734 remaining bodies were reburied in the Plot of the Unknown; later additions increased the number to 755. The following year, 777 white marble markers (a few extra markers were added for symmetry) were placed at the head of the graves.

On May 31, 1892, exactly three years after the Great Flood, the people of Johnstown and their guests officially dedicated the plot and the new Monument to the Unknown Dead. The impressive monument, sculpted from Vermont granite, towered twenty-one feet above the rows of gleaming white headstones. George Swank called the ceremony "the last public act of the tragedy of the Conemaugh." Nearly everyone in Johnstown attended. Various dignitaries gave eulogies to the victims and praised the survivors who had built a new city out of the ruins. The keynote speaker, Governor Robert Pattison, admonished those who might have the power to prevent such tragedy from ever happening again: "We who have to do with the concentrated forces of nature, the powers of air, electricity, water, steam, by careful forethought must leave nothing undone for the preservation and protection of the lives of our brother men."

The ceremony at Grand View marked the official closing of a tragic chapter in the history of Johnstown and the nation. But it took many years for the wounds to heal and the scars to disappear. Johnstown came through the ordeal, and by many accounts seemed stronger than before, but it paid a heavy toll. The crowd leaving Grand View formed a somber procession as people returned to the valley. The thoughts of many must have been on another cemetery procession, just three years earlier, on Memorial Day 1889—before the rain began to fall on the Valley of the Conemaugh.

The flood showed no mercy: it struck down young and old, man, woman, and child. One of the saddest stories is that of the Fenn family. The flood claimed the father and seven children. This portrait of six of the children is all that Mrs. Fenn had to remember them by. " 'John Fulton [age 12] was named in honor of the manager of the Cambria Iron Works, who took a great interest in him and made him a messenger boy when he grew old enough. . . . "Daisy" [age 10] . . . was a diligent scholar and . . . everybody liked her for her amiable ways. . . . George [age 8] was born on the anniversary of Washington's birthday and received the name of the father of his country. Anna's name [Anna Richmond Virginia, age 6] included my native city and state. The Germans were holding a celebration in Johnstown on the day my third son came into the world, so we decided to name him Bismarck. The baby was called Queen Esther [age 16 months] because the cantata by that name was produced on the evening of her birth. [Genevieve, age 9, was also lost.] If God had spared me *one* I could have been resigned. But all, all! Father in Heaven, is not my cross heavier than I can bear?' " [Mrs. Fenn, quoted in J. J. McLaurin]

Back cover
"We cannot help things by repining. We cannot bring the lost loved ones by giving way to our feelings which will now and again swell in spite of our endeavor to keep them down. But in the activities of business and industry we can find a solace and it is there we find it today. All eyes forward then. Look the other way." [George Swank, *Johnstown Tribune*, May 31, 1890]